everyday
baking

This edition published in 2010
LOVE FOOD is an imprint of Parragon Books Ltd

Parragon
Queen Street House
4 Queen Street
Bath BA1 1HE, UK

ISBN: 978-1-4075-6113-4

Printed in China

Designed by Terry Jeavons & Company

Notes for the Reader
This book uses both metric and imperial measurements. Follow the same units of measurement throughout; do not mix metric and imperial. All spoon measurements are level: teaspoons are assumed to be 5 ml, and tablespoons are assumed to be 15 ml. Unless otherwise stated, milk is assumed to be full fat, eggs and individual vegetables are medium, and pepper is freshly ground black pepper.

The times given are an approximate guide only. Preparation times differ according to the techniques used by different people and the cooking times may also vary from those given. Optional ingredients, variations or serving suggestions have not been included in the calculations.

Recipes using raw or very lightly cooked eggs should be avoided by infants, the elderly, pregnant women, convalescents and anyone suffering from an illness. Pregnant and breastfeeding women are advised to avoid eating peanuts and peanut products. Sufferers from nut allergies should be aware that some of the ready-made ingredients used in the recipes in this book may contain nuts. Always check the packaging before use.

everyday baking

introduction

Baking is without any doubt the most rewarding of culinary experiences. To mix together the most unpromising-looking collection of ingredients, put them in an oven and have them emerge as a truly delicious creation is nothing short of a miracle!

No wonder, then, that there is something of a mystery to the whole process that is often daunting to an inexperienced cook. In reality, however, it's nowhere near as difficult as it might appear to bake a sumptuous large cake, a melt-in-the-mouth muffin, your favourite pie, a loaf of bread to serve fresh from the oven or an elegant savoury tart – and these are just a few examples of the wonderful baking recipes you will find in this book.

There are several items of kitchen equipment that are worth investing in if you are planning to make baking a regular event. A selection of baking tins is a must – baking sheets and tart tins, as well as round and square cake tins of various sizes, including one or two of the 'springform' type to facilitate the removal of large cakes, tortes and cheesecakes.

Apart from this, a couple of generously sized mixing bowls, some wooden spoons and perhaps a hand-held electric mixer will be enough to get you started. A more expensive item of equipment that will pay for itself in no time is a multipurpose food mixer. The different attachments will enable you to mix cake batters and pastry, whisk egg whites, whip cream and knead bread dough with speed and efficiency. In the past, of course, cooks had no such gadgets to help them out, and there is a certain satisfaction in doing all of the above tasks by hand – kneading bread dough for ten minutes is guaranteed to relieve tension as well as produce a fabulous result.

Choose your favourite recipe, mix it with confidence and wait for the golden moment when you can bite into it!

cakes & gâteaux

Although a shop-bought cake is convenient and usually very good, a home-baked cake is so much better, perhaps because a little bit of the soul of the cook goes into it along with the other ingredients! If it doesn't come out looking absolutely perfect, it really doesn't matter – this just adds to its charm.

Different cakes suit different occasions, and you'll find a good cross-section here. For serving with morning coffee, try Gingerbread, Sticky Ginger Marmalade Loaf or Date & Walnut Loaf – these cakes improve with keeping, so can be wrapped in foil and stored in an airtight container for a few days. For an afternoon treat with tea, Sponge Cake, German Chocolate & Hazelnut Cake, Caribbean Coconut Cake, Honey Spiced Cake, Rich Fruit Cake and Banana & Lime Cake are perfect.

Some cakes make fabulous late-evening desserts – try a melting Torta de Cielo, fragrant Moroccan Orange & Almond Cake, moist Apple Streusel Cake or spicy Pear & Ginger Cake. Add a spoonful of whipped cream, ice cream, crème fraîche or thick yogurt, if you like.

And for those really special occasions? Chocolate Fudge Cake, Mocha Layer Cake, Coffee Caramel Cake, Chocolate Truffle Torte, Chocolate Cherry Layer Cake – you'll want to try them all!

chocolate fudge cake

ingredients

SERVES 8

175 g/6 oz unsalted butter, softened, plus extra for greasing
175 g/6 oz golden caster sugar
3 eggs, beaten
3 tbsp golden syrup
40 g/1½ oz ground almonds
175 g/6 oz self-raising flour
pinch of salt
40 g/1½ oz cocoa powder

icing

225 g/8 oz plain chocolate, broken into pieces
55 g/2 oz dark muscovado sugar
225 g/8 oz unsalted butter, diced
5 tbsp evaporated milk
½ tsp vanilla extract

method

1 Grease and line the bottom of 2 x 20-cm/8-inch round cake tins. To make the icing, place the chocolate, sugar, butter, evaporated milk and vanilla extract in a heavy-based pan. Heat gently, stirring constantly, until melted. Pour into a bowl and cool. Cover and chill in the refrigerator for 1 hour, or until spreadable.

2 Place the butter and sugar in a bowl and beat together until light and fluffy. Gradually beat in the eggs. Stir in the syrup and ground almonds. Sift the flour, salt and cocoa into a separate bowl, then fold into the mixture. Add a little water, if necessary, to make a dropping consistency. Spoon the mixture into the prepared tins and bake in a preheated oven, 180°C/350°F/Gas Mark 4, for 30–35 minutes, or until springy to the touch and a skewer inserted in the centre comes out clean.

3 Leave the cakes in the tins for 5 minutes, then turn out onto wire racks to cool completely. When the cakes are cold, sandwich them together with half the icing. Spread the remaining icing over the top and sides of the cake, swirling it to give a frosted appearance.

gingerbread

ingredients

SERVES 12–16

450 g/1 lb plain flour

3 tsp baking powder

1 tsp bicarbonate of soda

3 tsp ground ginger

175 g/6 oz butter

175 g/6 oz soft brown sugar

175 g/6 oz black treacle

175 g/6 oz golden syrup

1 egg, beaten

300 ml/10 fl oz milk

method

1 Line a 23-cm/9-inch square cake tin, 5 cm/2 inches deep, with baking paper.

2 Sift the flour, baking powder, bicarbonate of soda and ginger into a large mixing bowl.

3 Place the butter, sugar, treacle and syrup in a medium pan and heat over a low heat until the butter has melted and the sugar dissolved. Cool a little.

4 Mix the beaten egg with the milk and add to the cooled syrup mixture. Add the liquid ingredients to the flour mixture and beat well using a wooden spoon until the mixture is smooth and glossy.

5 Pour the mixture into the prepared tin and bake in the centre of a preheated oven, 160°C/325°F/Gas Mark 3, for 1½ hours until well risen and just firm to the touch.

6 Remove from the oven and cool in the tin. When cool, remove the cake from the tin with the lining paper. Overwrap with foil and place in an airtight container for up to 1 week to allow the flavours to mature. Cut into wedges to serve.

sticky ginger marmalade loaf

ingredients

SERVES 10

175 g/6 oz butter, softened, plus extra for greasing
125 g/4½ oz ginger marmalade
175 g/6 oz brown sugar
3 eggs, beaten
225 g/8 oz self-raising flour
½ tsp baking powder
1 tsp ground ginger
100 g/3½ oz coarsely chopped pecans

method

1 Grease and line the bottom and ends of a 900-g/2-lb loaf tin. Place 1 tablespoon of the ginger marmalade in a small pan and reserve. Place the remaining marmalade in a bowl with the butter, sugar and eggs.

2 Sift in the flour, baking powder and ground ginger and beat together until smooth. Stir in three-quarters of the nuts. Spoon the mixture into the prepared loaf tin and smooth the top. Sprinkle with the remaining nuts and bake in a preheated oven, 180°C/350°F/Gas Mark 4, for 1 hour, or until well risen and a skewer inserted into the centre comes out clean.

3 Cool in the tin for 10 minutes, then turn out and peel off the lining paper. Transfer to a wire rack to cool until warm. Set the pan of reserved marmalade over low heat to warm, then brush over the loaf and serve in slices.

carrot cake

ingredients

SERVES 16

2 eggs
175 g/6 oz molasses sugar
200 ml/7 fl oz sunflower oil
200 g/7 oz coarsely grated carrots
225 g/8 oz wholemeal flour
1 tsp baking soda
2 tsp ground cinnamon
whole nutmeg, grated (about 1 tsp)
115 g/4 oz roughly chopped walnuts

topping

115 g/4 oz half-fat cream cheese
4 tbsp butter, softened
85 g/3 oz icing sugar
1 tsp grated lemon rind
1 tsp grated orange rind

method

1 In a mixing bowl, beat the eggs until well blended and add the sugar and oil. Mix well. Add the grated carrot, sift in the flour, baking soda and spices, then add the walnuts. Mix everything together until well incorporated.

2 Grease and line a 20-cm/8-inch round cake tin. Spread the mixture into the prepared cake tin and bake in the centre of a preheated oven, 190°C/375°F/Gas Mark 5, for 40–50 minutes until the cake is nicely risen, firm to the touch and has begun to shrink away slightly from the edge of the tin. Remove from the oven and cool in the tin until just warm, then turn out onto a cooling rack.

3 To make the topping, put all the ingredients into a mixing bowl and beat together for 2–3 minutes until really smooth.

4 When the cake is completely cold, spread with the topping, smooth over with a palette knife, and allow to firm up a little before cutting into 16 portions. Store in an airtight container in a cool place for up to 1 week.

banana & chocolate loaf

ingredients

SERVES 8

115 g/4 oz butter, softened, plus extra for greasing
2 ripe bananas
85 g/3 oz golden caster sugar
2 eggs
200 g/7 oz self-raising flour
25 g/1 oz cocoa powder
1 tsp baking powder
1–2 tbsp milk
100 g/3½ oz plain chocolate chips
butter, to serve (optional)

method

1 Grease and line a 900-g/2-lb loaf tin. Peel the bananas and place in a large bowl. Mash with a fork.

2 Add the butter, sugar and eggs, then sift the flour, cocoa powder and baking powder into the bowl. Beat vigorously until smooth, adding enough milk to give a reluctant dropping consistency. Stir in the chocolate chips.

3 Spoon the mixture into the prepared tin and bake in a preheated oven, 180°C/350°F/Gas Mark 4, for 50–60 minutes, or until well risen and the tip of a knife inserted in the centre comes out clean. Let stand in the tin for 5 minutes, then turn out onto a wire rack to cool completely. Serve sliced, with or without butter.

date & walnut loaf

ingredients

SERVES 10

175 g/6 oz butter, plus extra for greasing
225 g/8 oz pitted dates, chopped into small pieces
grated rind and juice of 1 orange
50 ml/2 fl oz water
175 g/6 oz brown sugar
3 eggs, beaten
85 g/3 oz wholemeal self-raising flour
85 g/3 oz self-raising flour
55 g/2 oz chopped walnuts
8 walnut halves
orange zest, to decorate

method

1 Grease and line the bottom and ends of a 900-g/2-lb loaf tin. Place the dates in a pan with the orange rind and juice and water and cook over medium heat for 5 minutes, stirring, or until a soft purée has formed.

2 Place the butter and sugar in a bowl and beat together until light and fluffy. Gradually beat in the eggs, then sift in the flours and fold in with the chopped walnuts. Spread one-third of the mixture over the bottom of the prepared loaf tin and spread half the date purée over the top.

3 Repeat the layers, ending with the cake mixture. Arrange walnut halves on top. Bake in a preheated oven, 160°C/325°F/Gas Mark 3, for 1–1¼ hours, or until well risen and firm to the touch. Cool in the tin for 10 minutes. Turn out, peel off the lining paper and transfer to a wire rack to cool. Decorate with orange zest and serve in slices.

sponge cake

ingredients

SERVES 8–10

175 g/6 oz butter, at room temperature, plus extra for greasing
175 g/6 oz caster sugar
3 eggs, beaten
175 g/6 oz self-raising flour
pinch of salt

to serve

3 tbsp raspberry jam
1 tbsp caster or icing sugar

method

1 Grease 2 x 20-cm/8-inch round sponge cake tins and base-line with baking paper.

2 Beat the butter and sugar together in a mixing bowl using a wooden spoon or a hand-held mixer until the mixture is pale in colour and light and fluffy. Add the egg a little at a time, beating well after each addition.

3 Sift the flour and salt and carefully add to the mixture, folding it in with a metal spoon or a spatula. Divide the mixture between the tins and smooth over with the spatula. Place them on the same shelf in the centre of a preheated oven, 180°C/350°F/Gas Mark 4, and bake for 25–30 minutes until well risen, golden brown and beginning to shrink from the sides of the tins.

4 Remove from the oven and let stand for 1 minute. Loosen the cakes from around the edge of the tins using a round-bladed knife. Turn the cakes out onto a clean tea towel, remove the paper and invert them onto a wire rack (this prevents the wire rack from marking the top of the cakes). When completely cool, sandwich together with the jam and sprinkle with the sugar.

mocha layer cake

ingredients

SERVES 8

butter for greasing
200 g/7 oz self-raising flour
1/4 tsp baking powder
4 tbsp cocoa powder
100 g/3 1/2 oz caster sugar
2 eggs
2 tbsp golden syrup
150 ml/5 fl oz corn oil
150 ml/5 fl oz milk

filling

1 tsp instant coffee
1 tbsp boiling water
300 ml/10 fl oz double cream
2 tbsp icing sugar

to decorate

50 g/1 3/4 oz plain chocolate, grated
chocolate caraque
icing sugar, for dusting

method

1 Sift the flour, baking powder and cocoa into a large bowl, then stir in the sugar. Make a well in the centre and stir in the eggs, syrup, corn oil and milk. Beat with a wooden spoon, gradually mixing in the dry ingredients to make a smooth batter. Divide the mixture between 3 lightly greased 18-cm/7-inch cake tins.

2 Bake in a preheated oven, 180°C/350°F/Gas Mark 4, for 35–45 minutes, or until springy to the touch. Let stand in the tins for 5 minutes, then turn out and cool completely on a wire rack.

3 To make the filling, dissolve the instant coffee in the boiling water and place in a large bowl with the cream and icing sugar. Whip until the cream is just holding its shape, then use half the cream to sandwich the 3 cakes together. Spread the remaining cream over the top and sides of the cake. Press the grated chocolate into the cream round the edge of the cake.

4 Transfer the cake to a serving plate. Lay the chocolate caraque over the top of the cake. Cut a few thin strips of baking paper and place on top of the chocolate caraque. Dust lightly with icing sugar, then carefully remove the paper. Serve.

coffee caramel cake

ingredients

SERVES 8

175 g/6 oz butter, softened, plus extra for greasing
175 g/6 oz golden caster sugar
3 eggs, beaten
225 g/8 oz self-raising flour, sifted
100 ml/3½ fl oz strong black coffee
chocolate-covered coffee beans, to decorate

icing

125 ml/4 fl oz milk
125 g/4½ oz butter
3 tbsp golden caster sugar
575 g/1 lb 4½ oz icing sugar

method

1 Grease and base-line 2 x 20-cm/8-inch sponge cake tins. Place the butter and sugar in a bowl and beat together until light and fluffy. Gradually beat in the eggs, then fold in the flour and coffee. Divide the batter between the prepared tins and bake in a preheated oven, 180°C/350°F/Gas Mark 4, for 30 minutes, or until well risen and springy when pressed in the centre. Cool in the tins for 5 minutes, then turn out and peel off the lining paper. Transfer to wire racks to cool completely.

2 To make the icing, place the milk and butter in a pan, set over low heat and stir until the butter has melted. Remove the pan from the heat and set aside. Place the caster sugar in a separate, heavy-based pan and set over low heat, stirring constantly, until the sugar dissolves and turns a golden caramel. Remove from the heat and stir in the warm milk mixture. Return to the heat and stir until the caramel dissolves.

3 Remove from the heat and gradually stir in the icing sugar, beating until the icing is a smooth spreading consistency. Join the cakes together with some of the icing and spread the rest over the top and sides. Decorate with chocolate-covered coffee beans.

torta de cielo

ingredients

SERVES 4–6

225 g/8 oz unsalted butter, at room temperature, plus extra for greasing
175 g/6 oz whole almonds, in their skins
225 g/8 oz sugar
3 eggs, lightly beaten
1 tsp almond extract
1 tsp vanilla extract
9 tbsp plain flour
pinch of salt

to decorate

icing sugar, for dusting
slivered almonds, toasted

method

1 Lightly grease a 20-cm/8-inch round cake tin and line the tin with baking paper.

2 Place the almonds in a food processor and process to form a 'mealy' mixture. Set aside.

3 Beat the butter and sugar together in a large bowl until smooth and fluffy. Beat in the eggs, almonds and both the almond and vanilla extracts until well blended. Stir in the flour and salt and mix briefly, until the flour is just incorporated.

4 Pour or spoon the batter into the prepared tin and smooth the surface. Bake in a preheated oven, 180°C/350°F/Gas Mark 4, for 40–50 minutes, or until the cake feels spongy when gently pressed.

5 Remove from the oven and cool on a wire rack. To serve, dust with icing sugar and decorate with toasted slivered almonds.

chocolate truffle torte

ingredients

SERVES 10

butter, for greasing
55 g/2 oz golden caster sugar
2 eggs
25 g/1 oz plain flour
25 g/1 oz cocoa powder, plus extra to decorate
50 ml/2 fl oz cold strong black coffee
2 tbsp brandy

topping

600 ml/20 fl oz whipping cream
425 g/15 oz plain chocolate, melted and cooled
icing sugar, to decorate

method

1 Grease a 23-cm/9-inch springform cake tin with butter and line the bottom with baking paper. Place the sugar and eggs in a heatproof bowl and set over a pan of hot water. Whisk together until pale and mousse-like. Sift the flour and cocoa powder into a separate bowl, then fold gently into the cake batter. Pour into the prepared tin and bake in a preheated oven, 220°C/425°F/Gas Mark 7, for 7–10 minutes, or until risen and firm to the touch.

2 Transfer to a wire rack to cool. Wash and dry the tin and replace the cooled cake in the tin. Mix the coffee and brandy together and brush over the cake.

3 To make the topping, place the cream in a bowl and whip until very soft peaks form. Carefully fold in the cooled chocolate. Pour the chocolate mixture over the sponge and chill in the refrigerator for 4–5 hours, or until set.

4 To decorate the torte, sift cocoa powder over the top and remove carefully from the tin. Using strips of card or waxed paper as a mask, sift bands of icing sugar over the torte to create a striped pattern. To serve, cut into slices with a hot knife.

almond & hazelnut gâteau

ingredients

SERVES 8

butter, for greasing

4 eggs

100 g/3½ oz caster sugar

50 g/1¾ oz ground almonds

50 g/1¾ oz ground hazelnuts

5½ tbsp plain flour

50 g/1¾ oz flaked almonds

icing sugar, for dusting

filling

100 g/3½ oz plain chocolate

1 tbsp butter

300 ml/10 fl oz double cream

method

1 Whisk the eggs and caster sugar together for 10 minutes, or until light and foamy and the whisk leaves a trail that lasts a few seconds when lifted. Fold in the ground almonds and hazelnuts, sift the flour and fold in with a metal spoon or spatula. Pour into 2 lightly greased and base-lined 18-cm/7-inch round sponge cake tins.

2 Sprinkle the flaked almonds over the top of one of the cakes, then bake both cakes in a preheated oven, 190°C/375°F/Gas Mark 5, for 15–20 minutes, or until springy to the touch. Cool in the tins for 5 minutes, then turn out onto wire racks to cool completely.

3 To make the filling, melt the chocolate, remove from the heat and stir in the butter. Set aside until cool. Whip the cream until holding its shape, then fold in the chocolate until mixed.

4 Place the cake without the extra almonds on a serving plate and spread the filling over it. Allow to set slightly, then place the almond-topped cake on top of the filling and chill in the refrigerator for 1 hour. Dust with icing sugar and serve.

moroccan orange & almond cake

ingredients

SERVES 8

1 orange
115 g/4 oz butter, softened, plus extra for greasing
115 g/4 oz golden caster sugar
2 eggs, beaten
175 g/6 oz semolina
100 g/3½ oz ground almonds
1½ tsp baking powder
icing sugar, for dusting
strained plain yogurt, to serve

syrup

300 ml/10 fl oz orange juice
130 g/4¾ oz caster sugar
8 cardamom pods, crushed

method

1 Grate the rind from the orange, reserving some for the decoration, and squeeze the juice from one half. Place the butter, orange rind and sugar in a bowl and beat together until light and fluffy. Gradually beat in the eggs.

2 In a separate bowl, mix the semolina, ground almonds and baking powder, then fold into the creamed mixture with the orange juice. Spoon the batter into a greased and base-lined 20-cm/8-inch cake tin and bake in a preheated oven, 180°C/350°F/Gas Mark 4, for 30–40 minutes, or until well risen and a skewer inserted into the centre comes out clean. Cool in the tin for 10 minutes.

3 To make the syrup, place the orange juice, sugar and cardamom pods in a pan over low heat and stir until the sugar has dissolved. Bring to a boil and simmer for 4 minutes, or until syrupy.

4 Turn the cake out into a deep serving dish. Using a skewer, make holes over the surface of the warm cake. Strain the syrup into a separate bowl and spoon three-quarters of it over the cake, then set aside for 30 minutes. Dust the cake with icing sugar and cut into slices. Serve with the remaining syrup drizzled around, accompanied by strained plain yogurt decorated with the reserved orange rind.

german chocolate & hazelnut cake

ingredients

SERVES 8

175 g/6 oz unsalted butter, softened, plus extra for greasing
115 g/4 oz dark brown sugar
175 g/6 oz self-raising flour, plus extra for dusting
1 tbsp cocoa powder
1 tsp allspice
3 eggs, beaten
115 g/4 oz ground hazelnuts
2 tbsp black coffee
icing sugar, for dusting

method

1 Grease and flour a 19-cm/7½-inch kugelhopf tin. Place the butter and brown sugar in a large mixing bowl and beat together until light and fluffy. Sift the self-raising flour, cocoa powder and allspice into a separate bowl.

2 Beat the eggs into the creamed batter, one at a time, adding 1 tablespoon of the flour mixture with the second and third eggs. Fold in the remaining flour mixture, ground hazelnuts and coffee.

3 Turn into the prepared tin and bake in a preheated oven, 180°C/350°F/Gas Mark 4, for 45–50 minutes, or until the cake springs back when lightly pressed. Cool in the tin for 10 minutes, then turn out onto a wire rack to cool completely. Dust generously with icing sugar before serving.

caribbean coconut cake

ingredients

SERVES 8

280 g/10 oz butter, softened, plus extra for greasing
175 g/6 oz golden caster sugar
3 eggs
175 g/6 oz self-raising flour
1½ tsp baking powder
½ tsp freshly grated nutmeg
55 g/2 oz dry unsweetened coconut
5 tbsp coconut cream
280 g/10 oz icing sugar
5 tbsp pineapple jam
dry unsweetened coconut, toasted, to decorate

method

1 Grease and base-line 2 x 20-cm/8-inch sponge cake tins. Place 175 g/6 oz of the butter in a bowl with the sugar and eggs and sift in the flour, baking powder and nutmeg. Beat together until smooth, then stir in the coconut and 2 tablespoons of the coconut cream into the mixture.

2 Divide the mixture between the prepared tins and smooth the surface. Bake in a preheated oven, 180°C/350°F/Gas Mark 4, for 25 minutes, or until golden and firm to the touch. Cool in the tins for 5 minutes, then turn out onto a wire rack, peel off the lining paper and cool completely.

3 Sift the icing sugar into a bowl and add the remaining butter and coconut cream. Beat together until smooth. Spread the pineapple jam on one of the cakes and top with just under half of the buttercream. Place the other cake on top. Spread the remaining buttercream on top of the cake and scatter with the toasted coconut.

honey spiced cake

ingredients

SERVES 8

150 g/5½ oz butter, plus extra for greasing
115 g/4 oz brown sugar
175 g/6 oz honey
1 tbsp water
200 g/7 oz self-raising flour
½ tsp ground ginger
½ tsp ground cinnamon
½ tsp caraway seeds
seeds from 8 cardamom pods, ground
2 eggs, beaten
350 g/12 oz icing sugar

method

1 Grease a 1-litre/1¾-pint fluted cake tin. Place the butter, sugar, honey and water into a heavy-based pan. Set over low heat and stir until the butter has melted and the sugar has dissolved. Remove from the heat and cool for 10 minutes.

2 Sift the flour into a bowl and mix in the ginger, cinnamon, caraway seeds and cardamom. Make a well in the centre. Pour in the honey mixture and the eggs and beat well until smooth. Pour the batter into the prepared tin and bake in a preheated oven, 180°C/350°F/Gas Mark 4, for 40–50 minutes, or until well risen and a skewer inserted into the centre comes out clean. Cool in the tin for 5 minutes, then transfer to a wire rack to cool completely.

3 Sift the icing sugar into a bowl. Stir in enough warm water to make a smooth, flowing icing. Spoon over the cake, allowing it to flow down the sides, then allow to set.

rich chocolate cake

ingredients

SERVES 10–12

100 g/3½ oz raisins
finely grated rind and juice of 1 orange
175 g/6 oz butter, diced, plus extra for greasing
100 g/3½ oz plain chocolate, at least 70% cocoa solids, broken up
4 large eggs, beaten
100 g/3½ oz caster sugar
1 tsp vanilla extract
55 g/2 oz plain flour
55 g/2 oz ground almonds
½ tsp baking powder
pinch of salt
55 g/2 oz blanched almonds, toasted and chopped
icing sugar, sifted, to decorate

method

1 Put the raisins in a small bowl, add the orange juice and soak for 20 minutes. Line a deep 25-cm/10-inch round cake tin with a removable bottom with waxed paper and grease the paper; set aside.

2 Melt the butter and chocolate together in a small pan over medium heat, stirring. Remove from the heat and set aside to cool.

3 Using an electric mixer beat the eggs, sugar and vanilla together for about 3 minutes until light and fluffy. Stir in the cooled chocolate mixture.

4 Drain the raisins if they haven't absorbed all the orange juice. Sift over the flour, ground almonds, baking powder and salt. Add the raisins, orange rind and almonds and fold everything together.

5 Spoon into the cake tin and smooth the surface. Bake in a preheated oven, 180°C/350°F/Gas Mark 4, for about 40 minutes, or until a skewer inserted into the centre comes out clean and the cake starts to come away from the side of the tin. Cool in the tin for 10 minutes, then remove from the tin and cool completely on a wire rack. Dust with icing sugar before serving.

rich fruit cake

ingredients

SERVES 4

butter, for greasing
175 g/6 oz stoned unsweetened dates
125 g/4½ oz no-soak dried prunes
200 ml/7 fl oz unsweetened orange juice
2 tbsp treacle
1 tsp finely grated lemon rind
1 tsp finely grated orange rind
225 g/8 oz wholemeal self-raising flour
1 tsp mixed spice
125 g/4½ oz seedless raisins
125 g/4½ oz sultanas
125 g/4½ oz currants
125 g/4½ oz dried cranberries
3 large eggs, separated
1 tbsp apricot jam, warmed

icing

125 g/4½ oz icing sugar
1–2 tsp water
1 tsp vanilla extract
orange and lemon rind strips, to decorate

method

1 Grease and line a deep 20-cm/8-inch round cake tin. Chop the dates and prunes and place in a pan. Pour over the orange juice and simmer for 10 minutes. Remove the pan from the heat and beat the fruit mixture until puréed. Add the treacle and citrus rinds and cool.

2 Sift the flour and spice into a bowl, adding any bran that remains in the sieve. Add the dried fruits. When the date and prune mixture is cool, whisk in the egg yolks. Whisk the egg whites in a separate, clean bowl until stiff. Spoon the fruit mixture into the dry ingredients and mix together.

3 Gently fold in the egg whites. Transfer to the prepared tin and bake in a preheated oven, 160°C/325°F/Gas Mark 3, for 1½ hours. Cool in the tin.

4 Remove the cake from the tin and brush the top with jam. To make the icing, sift the sugar into a bowl and mix with enough water and the vanilla extract to form a soft icing. Spread the icing over the top of the cake and tidy the edges. Decorate with orange and lemon rind.

chocolate cherry layer cake

ingredients

SERVES 8

3 tbsp unsalted butter, melted, plus extra for greasing
900 g/2 lb fresh cherries, stoned and halved
250 g/9 oz caster sugar
100 ml/3½ fl oz cherry brandy
100 g/3½ oz plain flour
50 g/1¾ oz cocoa powder
½ tsp baking powder
4 eggs
1 litre/1¾ pints double cream
grated plain chocolate
whole fresh cherries, to decorate

method

1 Grease and line a 23-cm/9-inch springform cake tin. Put the halved cherries into a pan and add 3 tablespoons of the sugar and the cherry brandy. Simmer for 5 minutes. Strain, reserving the syrup. In another bowl, sift together the flour, cocoa and baking powder.

2 Put the eggs in a heatproof bowl and beat in 160 g/5¾ oz of the sugar. Place the bowl over a pan of simmering water and beat for 6 minutes until thickened. Remove from the heat, then gradually fold in the flour mixture and melted butter. Spoon into the cake tin. Bake in a preheated oven, 180°C/350°F/Gas Mark 4, for 40 minutes. Remove from the oven and cool.

3 Turn out the cake and cut in half horizontally. Whip the cream with the remaining sugar. Spread the reserved syrup over the cut sides of the cake. Arrange the cherries over one half, top with a layer of cream and place the other half on top. Cover with cream, press grated chocolate all over and decorate with cherries.

blueberry & lemon drizzle cake

ingredients

SERVES 12

225 g/8 oz butter, softened, plus extra for greasing
225 g/8 oz golden caster sugar
4 eggs, beaten
250 g/9 oz self-raising flour, sifted
finely grated rind and juice of 1 lemon
25 g/1 oz ground almonds
200 g/7 oz fresh blueberries

topping

juice of 2 lemons
115 g/4 oz golden caster sugar

method

1 Grease and line the bottom of a 20-cm/ 8-inch square cake tin. Place the butter and sugar in a bowl and beat together until light and fluffy. Gradually beat in the eggs, adding a little flour toward the end to prevent curdling. Beat in the lemon rind, then fold in the remaining flour and almonds with enough of the lemon juice to give a good dropping consistency.

2 Fold in three-quarters of the blueberries and turn into the prepared tin. Smooth the surface, then scatter the remaining blueberries on top. Bake in a preheated oven, 180°C/350°F/ Gas Mark 4, for 1 hour, or until firm to the touch and a skewer inserted into the centre comes out clean.

3 To make the topping, place the lemon juice and sugar in a bowl and mix together. As soon as the cake comes out of the oven, prick it all over with a fine skewer and pour over the lemon mixture. Cool in the tin until completely cold, then cut into 12 squares to serve.

apple streusel cake

ingredients

SERVES 8

115 g/4 oz butter, plus extra for greasing
450 g/1 lb tart cooking apples
175 g/6 oz self-raising flour
1 tsp ground cinnamon
pinch of salt
115 g/4 oz golden caster sugar
2 eggs
1–2 tbsp milk
icing sugar, for dusting

streusel topping

115 g/4 oz self-raising flour
6 tbsp butter
85 g/3 oz golden caster sugar

method

1 Grease a 23-cm/9-inch springform cake tin. To make the streusel topping, sift the flour into a bowl and rub in the butter until the mixture resembles coarse crumbs. Stir in the sugar and set aside.

2 Peel, core and thinly slice the apples. To make the cake, sift the flour into a bowl with the cinnamon and salt. Place the butter and sugar in a separate bowl and beat together until light and fluffy. Gradually beat in the eggs, adding a little of the flour mixture with the last addition of egg. Gently fold in half the remaining flour mixture, then fold in the rest with the milk.

3 Spoon the batter into the prepared tin and smooth the top. Cover with the sliced apples and sprinkle the streusel topping evenly over the top. Bake in a preheated oven, 180°C/350°F/Gas Mark 4, for 1 hour, or until browned and firm to the touch. Cool in the tin before opening the sides. Dust the cake with icing sugar before serving.

banana & lime cake

ingredients

SERVES 10

butter, for greasing
300 g/10½ oz plain flour
1 tsp salt
1½ tsp baking powder
175 g/6 oz brown sugar
1 tsp grated lime rind
1 egg, beaten
1 banana, mashed with 1 tbsp lime juice
150 ml/5 fl oz low-fat cream cheese
115 g/4 oz sultanas

topping

115 g/4 oz icing sugar
1–2 tsp lime juice
½ tsp finely grated lime rind

to decorate

banana chips
finely grated lime rind

method

1 Grease and line a deep 18-cm/7-inch round cake tin with baking paper. Sift the flour, salt and baking powder into a large bowl and stir in the sugar and lime rind.

2 Make a well in the centre of the dry ingredients and add the egg, banana, cream cheese and sultanas. Mix well until thoroughly incorporated. Spoon the batter into the tin and smooth the surface.

3 Bake in a preheated oven, 180°C/350°F/Gas Mark 4, for 40–45 minutes, until firm to the touch or until a skewer inserted in the centre comes out clean. Cool the cake in the tin for 10 minutes, then turn out onto a wire rack to cool completely.

4 To make the topping, sift the icing sugar into a small bowl and mix with the lime juice to form a soft, but not too runny icing. Stir in the grated lime rind. Drizzle the icing over the cake, letting it run down the sides. Decorate the cake with banana chips and lime rind. Allow the cake to stand for 15 minutes so that the icing sets.

pear & ginger cake

ingredients

SERVES 6

200 g/7 oz unsalted butter, softened, plus extra for greasing
175 g/6 oz caster sugar
175 g/6 oz self-raising flour, sifted
1 tbsp ground ginger
3 eggs, beaten lightly
450 g/1 lb pears, peeled, cored and thinly sliced, then brushed with lemon juice
1 tbsp brown sugar
ice cream or double cream, lightly whipped, to serve (optional)

method

1 Lightly grease a deep 20-cm/8-inch cake tin with butter and line the bottom with baking paper.

2 Mix all but 2 tablespoons of the butter with the caster sugar, flour, ginger and eggs in a bowl. Beat with a whisk until the mixture forms a smooth consistency.

3 Spoon the cake batter into the prepared tin and level out the surface with a spatula. Arrange the pear slices over the cake batter. Sprinkle with the brown sugar and dot with the remaining butter.

4 Bake in a preheated oven, 180°C/350°F/Gas Mark 4, for 35–40 minutes, or until the cake is golden on top and feels springy to the touch. Serve warm, with ice cream or whipped cream, if you like.

small bites

Small bites – muffins, cupcakes, biscuits and slices – have a very special appeal, perhaps because they have a delightfully self-indulgent, 'just for me' feel about them!

Children love small bites, so they'll be thrilled to find a treat in their school lunchbox – a Drizzled Honey Cupcake, Apple & Cinnamon Muffin, Spiced Chocolate Muffin, Fruit & Nut Square or an Oat & Hazelnut Bite or two will revive them after the morning's exertions and set them up for the afternoon. When they get home from school, let them get their fingers sticky with an Iced Peanut Butter Cupcake, Sticky Gingerbread Cupcake, Banana & Pecan Cupcake or a Lemon Butterfly Cake – gorgeously messy!

Grown-ups – probably as an antidote to being grown up – love anything with a hint of wickedness and preferably more than a hint of chocolate! Devil's Food Cakes with Chocolate Icing, Chocolate Temptations and Warm Molten-centred Chocolate Cupcakes are satisfyingly naughty.

For more sedate adult occasions, Fudge Nut Muffins, Fig & Almond Muffins, Lavender Biscuits and Fig & Walnut Cookies are simply delicious, and a Rose Petal Cupcake, with its delicate pink icing, is a thoughtful treat to serve on a birthday or anniversary.

drizzled honey cupcakes

ingredients

SERVES 12

85 g/3 oz self-raising flour
1/4 tsp ground cinnamon
pinch of ground cloves
pinch of grated nutmeg
6 tbsp butter, softened
85 g/3 oz caster sugar
1 tbsp honey
finely grated rind of 1 orange
2 eggs, lightly beaten
40 g/1 1/2 oz walnut pieces, chopped

topping

15 g/1/2 oz walnut pieces, chopped
1/4 tsp ground cinnamon
2 tbsp honey
juice of 1 orange

method

1 Put 12 paper baking cases in a muffin tin, or place 12 double-layer paper cases on a baking sheet.

2 Sift the flour, cinnamon, cloves and nutmeg together into a bowl. Put the butter and sugar in a separate bowl and beat together until light and fluffy. Beat in the honey and orange rind, then gradually add the eggs, beating well after each addition. Using a metal spoon, fold in the flour mixture. Stir in the walnuts, then spoon the batter into the paper cases.

3 Bake the cupcakes in a preheated oven, 190°C/375°F/Gas Mark 5, for 20 minutes, or until well risen and golden brown. Transfer to a wire rack to cool.

4 To make the topping, mix together the walnuts and cinnamon. Put the honey and orange juice in a pan and heat gently, stirring, until combined.

5 When the cupcakes have almost cooled, prick the tops all over with a fork or skewer and then drizzle with the warm honey mixture. Sprinkle the walnut mixture over the top of each cupcake and serve warm or cold.

iced peanut butter cupcakes

ingredients

SERVES 16

4 tbsp butter, softened, or soft margarine
225 g/8 oz brown sugar
115 g/4 oz crunchy peanut butter
2 eggs, lightly beaten
1 tsp vanilla extract
225 g/8 oz plain flour
2 tsp baking powder
100 ml/3½ fl oz milk

icing

200 g/7 oz full-fat soft cream cheese
2 tbsp butter, softened
225 g/8 oz icing sugar

method

1 Put 16 muffin paper cases in a muffin tin.

2 Put the butter, sugar and peanut butter in a bowl and beat together for 1–2 minutes, or until well mixed. Gradually add the eggs, beating well after each addition, then add the vanilla extract. Sift in the flour and baking powder and then, using a metal spoon, fold them into the mixture, alternating with the milk. Spoon the batter into the paper cases.

3 Bake the cupcakes in a preheated oven, 180°C/350°F/Gas Mark 4, for 25 minutes, or until well risen and golden brown. Transfer to a wire rack to cool.

4 To make the icing, put the cream cheese and butter in a large bowl and, using an electric hand whisk, beat together until smooth. Sift the icing sugar into the mixture, then beat together until well mixed.

5 When the cupcakes are cold, spread the icing on top of each cupcake, swirling it with a round-bladed knife. Store the cupcakes in the refrigerator until ready to serve.

rose petal cupcakes

ingredients

SERVES 12

8 tbsp butter, softened
115 g/4 oz caster sugar
2 eggs, lightly beaten
1 tbsp milk
few drops of extract of rose oil
1/4 tsp vanilla extract
175 g/6 oz self-raising flour

icing

6 tbsp butter, softened
175 g/6 oz icing sugar
pink or purple food colouring (optional)
silver dragées (cake decoration balls), to decorate

candied rose petals

12–24 rose petals
lightly beaten egg white, for brushing
caster sugar, for sprinkling

method

1 To make the candied rose petals, gently rinse the petals and dry well with kitchen paper. Using a pastry brush, paint both sides of a rose petal with egg white, then coat well with caster sugar. Place on a tray and repeat with the remaining petals. Cover the tray with foil and set aside to dry overnight.

2 Put 12 paper baking cases in a muffin tin, or place 12 double-layer paper cases on a baking sheet.

3 Put the butter and sugar in a bowl and beat together until light and fluffy. Gradually add the eggs, beating well after each addition. Stir in the milk, rose oil extract and vanilla extract then, using a metal spoon, fold in the flour. Spoon the batter into the paper cases.

4 Bake the cupcakes in a preheated oven, 200°C/400°F/Gas Mark 6, for 12–15 minutes until well risen and golden brown. Transfer to a wire rack to cool.

5 To make the icing, put the butter in a large bowl and beat until fluffy. Sift in the icing sugar and mix well together. If wished, add a few drops of pink or purple food colouring to complement the rose petals.

6 When the cupcakes are cold, spread the icing on top of each cake. Top with 1–2 candied rose petals and sprinkle with silver dragées to decorate.

sticky gingerbread cupcakes

ingredients

SERVES 16

115 g/4 oz plain flour
2 tsp ground ginger
3/4 tsp ground cinnamon
1 piece preserved ginger, finely chopped
3/4 tsp bicarbonate of soda
4 tbsp milk
6 tbsp butter, softened, or soft margarine
70 g/2 1/2 oz brown sugar
2 tbsp treacle
2 eggs, lightly beaten
pieces of preserved ginger, to decorate

icing

6 tbsp butter, softened
175 g/6 oz icing sugar
2 tbsp ginger syrup from the preserved ginger jar

method

1 Put 16 paper baking cases in a muffin tin, or place 16 double-layer paper cases on a baking sheet.

2 Sift the flour, ground ginger and cinnamon together into a bowl. Add the chopped ginger and toss in the flour mixture until well coated. In a separate bowl, dissolve the bicarbonate of soda in the milk.

3 Put the butter and sugar in a bowl and beat together until fluffy. Beat in the treacle, then gradually add the eggs, beating well after each addition. Beat in the flour mixture, then gradually beat in the milk. Spoon the batter into the paper cases.

4 Bake the cupcakes in a preheated oven, 160°C/325°F/Gas Mark 3, for 20 minutes, or until well risen and golden brown. Transfer to a wire rack to cool.

5 To make the icing, put the butter in a bowl and beat until fluffy. Sift in the sugar, add the ginger syrup and beat together until smooth and creamy. Slice the preserved ginger into thin slivers or chop finely.

6 When the cupcakes are cold, spread the icing on top of each cupcake, then decorate with pieces of ginger.

fudge nut muffins

ingredients

SERVES 12

250 g/9 oz plain flour
4 tsp baking powder
85 g/3 oz caster sugar
6 tbsp crunchy peanut butter
1 large egg, beaten
4 tbsp butter, melted
175 ml/6 fl oz milk
150 g/5½ oz vanilla fudge, cut into small pieces
3 tbsp coarsely chopped unsalted peanuts

method

1 Line a 12-cup muffin tin with double muffin paper liners. Sift the flour and baking powder into a bowl. Stir in the caster sugar. Add the peanut butter and stir until the mixture resembles breadcrumbs.

2 Place the egg, butter and milk in a separate bowl and beat until blended, then stir into the dry ingredients until just blended. Lightly stir in the fudge pieces. Divide the batter evenly between the muffin liners.

3 Sprinkle the chopped peanuts on top and bake in a preheated oven, 200°C/400°F/Gas Mark 6, for 20–25 minutes until well risen and firm to the touch. Remove the muffins from the oven and cool for 2 minutes, then place them on a wire rack to cool completely.

fig & almond muffins

ingredients

SERVES 12

- 2 tbsp sunflower or peanut oil, plus extra for oiling (if using)
- 250 g/9 oz plain flour
- 1 tsp baking soda
- 1/2 tsp salt
- 225 g/8 oz raw sugar
- 85 g/3 oz dried figs, chopped
- 115 g/4 oz almonds, chopped
- 200 ml/7 fl oz water
- 1 tsp almond extract
- 2 tbsp chopped almonds, to decorate

method

1 Oil a 12-cup muffin tin with sunflower oil, or line it with 12 muffin paper liners. Sift the flour, baking soda and salt into a mixing bowl, then add the raw sugar and stir together.

2 In a separate bowl, mix the figs, almonds and sunflower oil together, then stir in the water and almond extract. Add the fruit and nut mixture to the flour mixture and gently stir together. Do not overstir – it is fine for it to be a little lumpy.

3 Divide the muffin batter evenly between the 12 cups in the muffin tin or the paper liners (they should be about two-thirds full), then sprinkle over the remaining chopped almonds to decorate. Transfer to a preheated oven, 190°C/375°F/Gas Mark 5 and bake for 25 minutes, or until risen and golden.

4 Remove the muffins from the oven and serve warm, or place them on a wire rack to cool.

banana & pecan cupcakes

ingredients

SERVES 12

225 g/8 oz plain flour
$1^1/_4$ tsp baking powder
$^1/_4$ tsp bicarbonate of soda
2 ripe bananas
8 tbsp butter, softened, or soft margarine
115 g/4 oz caster sugar
$^1/_2$ tsp vanilla extract
2 eggs, lightly beaten
4 tbsp soured cream
55 g/2 oz pecans, coarsely chopped

topping

8 tbsp butter, softened
115 g/4 oz icing sugar
25 g/1 oz pecans, chopped

method

1 Line a 12-cup muffin tin with a double layer of muffin paper liners, or place 12 double-layer paper cases on a baking sheet.

2 Sift together the flour, baking powder and bicarbonate of soda. Peel the bananas, put them in a bowl and mash with a fork.

3 Put the butter, sugar and vanilla in a bowl and beat together until light and fluffy. Gradually add the eggs, beating well after each addition. Stir in the mashed bananas and soured cream. Using a metal spoon, fold in the sifted flour mixture and the chopped nuts, then spoon the batter into the paper cases.

4 Bake the cupcakes in a preheated oven, 190°C/375°F/Gas Mark 5, for 20 minutes, or until well risen and golden brown. Transfer to a wire rack to cool.

5 To make the topping, beat the butter in a bowl until fluffy. Sift in the icing sugar and mix together well. Spread the icing on top of each cupcake and sprinkle with the chopped pecans before serving.

apple & cinnamon muffins

ingredients

SERVES 6

85 g/3 oz plain wholemeal flour
70 g/2½ oz plain flour
1½ tsp baking powder
pinch of salt
1 tsp ground cinnamon
40 g/1½ oz golden caster sugar
2 small eating apples, peeled, cored and finely chopped
125 ml/4 fl oz milk
1 egg, beaten
4 tbsp butter, melted

topping

12 brown sugar lumps, coarsely crushed
½ tsp ground cinnamon

method

1 Place 6 muffin paper liners in a muffin tin.

2 Sift both flours, baking powder, salt and cinnamon together into a large bowl and stir in the sugar and chopped apples. Place the milk, egg and butter in a separate bowl and mix. Add the wet ingredients to the dry ingredients and gently stir until just combined.

3 Divide the batter evenly between the paper liners. To make the topping, mix the crushed sugar lumps and cinnamon together and sprinkle over the muffins. Bake in a preheated oven, 200°C/400°F/ Gas Mark 6, for 20–25 minutes, or until well risen and golden. Remove the muffins from the oven and serve warm or place them on a wire rack to cool.

moist walnut cupcakes

ingredients

SERVES 12

85 g/3 oz walnuts
4 tbsp butter, softened
100 g/3½ oz caster sugar
grated rind of ½ lemon
70 g/2½ oz self-raising flour
2 eggs
12 walnut halves, to decorate

icing

4 tbsp butter, softened
85 g/3 oz icing sugar
grated rind of ½ lemon
1 tsp lemon juice

method

1 Put 12 paper baking cases in a muffin tin, or place 12 double-layer paper cases on a baking sheet.

2 Put the walnuts in a food processor and, using a pulsating action, blend until finely ground, being careful not to overgrind, which will turn them to oil. Add the butter, cut into small pieces, along with the sugar, lemon rind, flour and eggs, then blend until evenly mixed. Spoon the batter into the paper cases.

3 Bake the cupcakes in a preheated oven, 190°C/375°F/Gas Mark 5, for 20 minutes, or until well risen and golden brown. Transfer to a wire rack to cool.

4 To make the icing, put the butter in a bowl and beat until fluffy. Sift in the icing sugar, add the lemon rind and juice and mix well.

5 When the cupcakes are cold, spread the icing on top of each cupcake and top with a walnut to decorate.

walnut & cinnamon blondies

ingredients

SERVES 9

115 g/4 oz butter, plus extra for greasing
225 g/8 oz brown sugar
1 egg
1 egg yolk
150 g/5 oz self-raising flour
1 tsp ground cinnamon
85 g/3 oz coarsely chopped walnuts

method

1 Grease and base-line an 18-cm/7-in square cake tin. Place the butter and sugar in a pan over low heat and stir until the sugar has dissolved. Cook, stirring, for a further 1 minute. The mixture will bubble slightly, but do not let it boil. Cool for 10 minutes.

2 Stir the egg and egg yolk into the mixture. Sift in the flour and cinnamon, add the nuts and stir until just blended. Pour the cake batter into the prepared cake tin, then bake in a preheated oven, 180°C/350°F/Gas Mark 4, for 20–25 minutes, or until springy in the centre and a skewer inserted into the centre of the cake comes out clean.

3 Cool in the tin for a few minutes, then run a knife round the edge of the cake to loosen it. Turn the cake out onto a wire rack and peel off the paper. Cool completely. When cold, cut into squares.

lemon butterfly cakes

ingredients

SERVES 12

115 g/4 oz self-raising flour
1/2 tsp baking powder
8 tbsp soft margarine
115 g/4 oz caster sugar
2 eggs, lightly beaten
finely grated rind of 1/2 lemon
2 tbsp milk
icing sugar, for dusting

lemon filling

6 tbsp butter, softened
175 g/6 oz icing sugar
1 tbsp lemon juice

method

1 Put 12 paper baking cases in a muffin tin, or place 12 double-layer paper cases on a baking sheet.

2 Sift the flour and baking powder into a large bowl. Add the margarine, sugar, eggs, lemon rind and milk and, using an electric hand whisk, beat together until smooth. Spoon the batter into the paper cases.

3 Bake the cupcakes in a preheated oven, 190°C/375°F/Gas Mark 5, for 15–20 minutes, or until well risen and golden brown. Transfer to a wire rack to cool.

4 To make the filling, put the butter in a bowl and beat until fluffy. Sift in the icing sugar, add the lemon juice and beat together until smooth and creamy.

5 When the cupcakes are cold, use a serrated knife to cut a circle from the top of each cupcake and then cut each circle in half. Spread or pipe a little of the buttercream filling into the centre of each cupcake, then press the 2 semicircular halves into it at an angle to resemble butterfly wings. Dust the cakes with sifted icing sugar before serving.

warm molten-centred chocolate cupcakes

ingredients

SERVES 8

4 tbsp soft margarine
55 g/2 oz caster sugar
1 large egg
85 g/3 oz self-raising flour
1 tbsp cocoa powder
55 g/2 oz plain chocolate
icing sugar, for dusting

method

1 Put 8 paper baking cases in a muffin tin, or place 8 double-layer paper cases on a baking sheet.

2 Put the margarine, sugar, egg, flour and cocoa in a large bowl and, using an electric hand whisk, beat together until just smooth.

3 Spoon half of the batter into the paper cases. Using a teaspoon, make an indentation in the centre of each cake. Break the chocolate evenly into 8 squares and place a piece in each indentation, then spoon the remaining cake batter on top.

4 Bake the cupcakes in a preheated oven, 190ºC/375ºF/Gas Mark 5, for 20 minutes, or until well risen and springy to the touch. Leave the cupcakes for 2–3 minutes before serving warm, dusted with sifted icing sugar.

spiced chocolate muffins

ingredients

SERVES 12

100 g/3½ oz butter, softened
150 g/5 oz caster sugar
115 g/4 oz brown sugar
2 large eggs
150 ml/5 fl oz soured cream
5 tbsp milk
250 g/9 oz plain flour
1 tsp baking soda
2 tbsp cocoa powder
1 tsp allspice
200 g/7 oz plain chocolate chips

method

1 Line a 12-cup muffin tin with muffin liners.

2 Place the butter, caster sugar and brown sugar in a bowl and beat well. Beat in the eggs, soured cream and milk until thoroughly mixed. Sift the flour, baking soda, cocoa and allspice into a separate bowl and stir into the mixture. Add the chocolate chips and mix well. Divide the batter evenly between the paper liners. Bake in a preheated oven, 190°C/375°F/Gas Mark 5, for 25–30 minutes.

3 Remove from the oven and cool for 10 minutes. Place them on a wire rack to cool completely. Store in an airtight container until required.

devil's food cakes with chocolate icing

ingredients

SERVES 18

3½ tbsp soft margarine
115 g/4 oz brown sugar
2 large eggs
115 g/4 oz plain flour
½ tsp baking soda
25 g/1 oz cocoa powder
125 ml/4 fl oz soured cream

icing

125 g/4½ oz plain chocolate
2 tbsp caster sugar
150 ml/5 fl oz soured cream

chocolate curls

(optional)
100 g/3½ oz plain chocolate

method

1 Put 18 paper baking cases in a muffin tin, or put 18 double-layer paper cases on a baking sheet.

2 Put the margarine, sugar, eggs, flour, baking soda and cocoa in a large bowl and, using an electric hand whisk, beat together until just smooth. Using a metal spoon, fold in the soured cream. Spoon the batter into the paper cases.

3 Bake the cupcakes in a preheated oven, 180°C/350°F/Gas Mark 4, for 20 minutes, or until well risen and firm to the touch. Transfer to a wire rack to cool.

4 To make the icing, break the chocolate into a heatproof bowl. Set the bowl over a pan of gently simmering water and heat until melted, stirring occasionally. Remove from the heat and cool slightly, then whisk in the sugar and soured cream until combined. Spread the icing over the tops of the cupcakes and allow to set in the refrigerator before serving. If liked, serve decorated with chocolate curls made by shaving plain chocolate with a potato peeler.

fruit & nut squares

ingredients

SERVES 9

115 g/4 oz unsalted butter, plus extra for greasing
2 tbsp honey
1 egg, beaten
85 g/3 oz ground almonds
115 g/4 oz no-soak dried apricots, finely chopped
55 g/2 oz dried cherries
55 g/2 oz toasted chopped hazelnuts
25 g/1 oz sesame seeds
85 g/3 oz rolled oats

method

1 Lightly grease an 18-cm/7-inch shallow, square baking tin with butter. Beat the remaining butter with the honey in a bowl until creamy, then beat in the egg with the almonds.

2 Add the remaining ingredients and mix together. Press into the prepared tin, ensuring that the mixture is firmly packed, and smooth the surface.

3 Bake in a preheated oven, 180°C/350°F/Gas Mark 4, for 20–25 minutes, or until firm to the touch and golden brown.

4 Remove from the oven and let stand for 10 minutes before marking into squares. Cool completely before removing from the tin. Store in an airtight container.

pecan brownies

ingredients

SERVES 20

225 g/8 oz unsalted butter, plus extra for greasing
70 g/2½ oz plain chocolate
125 g/4½ oz plain flour
¾ tsp bicarbonate of soda
¼ tsp baking powder
55 g/2 oz pecans
100 g/3½ oz demerara sugar
½ tsp almond extract
1 egg
1 tsp milk

method

1 Grease a large baking tin and line it with baking paper.

2 Put the chocolate in a heatproof bowl set over a pan of gently simmering water and heat until it is melted. Meanwhile, sift together the flour, bicarbonate of soda and baking powder into a large bowl.

3 Finely chop the pecans and set aside. In a separate bowl, cream together the butter and sugar, then mix in the almond extract and the egg. Remove the chocolate from the heat and stir into the butter mixture. Add the flour mixture, milk and chopped nuts to the bowl and stir until well combined.

4 Spoon the mixture into the prepared baking tin and smooth it. Transfer to a preheated oven, 180°C/350°F/Gas Mark 4, and cook for 30 minutes, or until firm to the touch (it should still be a little soft in the centre). Remove from the oven and cool completely. Cut into 20 squares and serve.

white chocolate brownies

ingredients

SERVES 9

115 g/4 oz unsalted butter, plus extra for greasing
225 g/8 oz white chocolate
115 g/4 oz walnut pieces
2 eggs
115 g/4 oz soft brown sugar
115 g/4 oz self-raising flour

method

1 Lightly grease an 18-cm/7-inch square cake tin with butter.

2 Coarsely chop 175 g/6 oz of chocolate and all the walnuts. Put the remaining chocolate and the butter in a heatproof bowl set over a pan of gently simmering water. When melted, stir together, then set aside to cool slightly.

3 Whisk the eggs and sugar together, then beat in the cooled chocolate mixture until well mixed. Fold in the flour, chopped chocolate and the walnuts. Turn the mixture into the prepared tin and smooth the surface.

4 Transfer the tin to a preheated oven, 180°C/350°F/Gas Mark 4, and bake for 30 minutes, or until just set. The mixture should still be a little soft in the centre. Remove from the oven and cool in the tin, then cut into 9 squares before serving.

chocolate temptations

ingredients

SERVES 24

- 365 g/12½ oz plain chocolate
- 6 tbsp unsalted butter, plus extra for greasing
- 1 tsp strong coffee
- 2 eggs
- 150 g/5 oz soft brown sugar
- 225 g/8 oz plain flour
- ¼ tsp baking powder
- pinch of salt
- 2 tsp almond extract
- 50 g/1¾ oz Brazil nuts, chopped
- 50 g/1¾ oz hazelnuts, chopped
- 40 g/1½ oz white chocolate

method

1 Put 225 g/8 oz of the plain chocolate with the butter and coffee into a heatproof bowl over a pan of simmering water and heat until the chocolate is almost melted.

2 Meanwhile, beat the eggs in a bowl until fluffy. Whisk in the sugar gradually until thick. Remove the chocolate from the heat and stir until smooth. Stir it into the egg mixture until combined.

3 Sift the flour, baking powder and salt into a bowl and stir into the chocolate mixture. Chop 85 g/3 oz of plain chocolate into pieces and stir into the dough. Stir in the almond extract and nuts.

4 Put 24 rounded dessertspoonfuls of the dough on a greased baking sheet and bake in a preheated oven, 180°C/350°F/Gas Mark 4, for 16 minutes. Transfer the cookies to a wire rack to cool. To decorate, melt the remaining chocolate (plain and white) in turn, then spoon into a piping bag and pipe lines onto the cookies.

chocolate chip oat cookies

ingredients

SERVES 20

115 g/4 oz butter, softened, plus extra for greasing
115 g/4 oz light brown sugar
1 egg
100 g/3½ oz rolled oats
1 tbsp milk
1 tsp vanilla extract
125 g/4½ oz plain flour
1 tbsp cocoa powder
½ tsp baking powder
175 g/6 oz plain chocolate, broken into pieces
175 g/6 oz milk chocolate, broken into pieces

method

1 Place the butter and sugar in a bowl and beat together until light and fluffy. Beat in the egg, then add the oats, milk and vanilla extract. Beat together until well blended. Sift the flour, cocoa powder and baking powder into the cookie dough and stir. Stir in the chocolate pieces.

2 Place dessertspoonfuls of the cookie dough on 2 greased baking sheets and flatten slightly with a fork. Bake in a preheated oven, 180°C/350°F/Gas Mark 4, for 15 minutes, or until slightly risen and firm. Cool on the baking sheets for 2 minutes, then transfer to wire racks to cool completely.

lavender biscuits

ingredients

SERVES 12

55 g/2 oz golden caster sugar
1 tsp chopped lavender leaves
115 g/4 oz butter, softened, plus extra for greasing
finely grated rind of 1 lemon
175 g/6 oz plain flour

method

1 Place the sugar and lavender leaves in a food processor. Process until the lavender is very finely chopped, then add the butter and lemon rind and process until light and fluffy. Transfer to a large bowl. Sift in the flour and beat until the mixture forms a stiff dough.

2 Place the dough on a sheet of baking paper and place another sheet on top. Gently press down with a rolling pin and roll out to 3–5 mm/ 1/8–1/4 inch thick. Remove the top sheet of paper and stamp out circles from the dough using a 7-cm/2 3/4-inch round biscuit cutter. Re-knead and re-roll the dough trimmings and stamp out more biscuits.

3 Using a spatula, carefully transfer the biscuits to a large, greased baking sheet. Prick the biscuits with a fork and bake in a preheated oven, 150°C/300°F/Gas Mark 2, for 12 minutes, or until pale golden brown. Cool on the baking sheet for 2 minutes, then transfer to a wire rack to cool completely.

fig & walnut cookies

ingredients

SERVES 20

100 g/3½ oz dried figs
225 g/8 oz unsalted butter or margarine, plus extra for greasing
125 ml/4 fl oz clear honey
4 tbsp raw brown sugar
2 eggs, beaten
pinch of salt
1 tsp allspice
1 tsp bicarbonate of soda
½ tsp vanilla extract
2 tbsp dried dates, finely chopped
225 g/8 oz plain flour
225 g/8 oz oats
25 g/1 oz walnuts, finely chopped
dried fig pieces, to decorate (optional)

method

1 Finely chop the figs. Mix the butter, honey, figs and sugar together in a large bowl. Beat the eggs into the mixture and mix thoroughly.

2 In a separate bowl, combine the salt, allspice, bicarbonate of soda, vanilla extract and dates. Gradually stir them into the creamed mixture. Sift the flour into the mixture and stir well. Finally, mix in the oats and walnuts.

3 Drop 20 rounded tablespoonfuls of the mixture onto 2 large greased baking sheets, spaced well apart to allow for spreading. Decorate with fig pieces, if using. Bake in a preheated oven, 180°C/350°F/Gas Mark 4, for 10–15 minutes, or until the cookies are golden brown. Remove from the oven. Transfer to a wire rack and cool completely before serving.

oat & hazelnut bites

ingredients

SERVES 30

175 g/6 oz unsalted butter or margarine, plus extra for greasing
225 g/8 oz raw brown sugar
1 egg, beaten
4 tbsp milk
1 tsp vanilla extract
1/2 tsp almond extract
115 g/4 oz hazelnuts
115 g/4 oz plain flour
1 1/2 tsp ground allspice
1/4 tsp bicarbonate of soda
pinch of salt
225 g/8 oz oats
150 g/5 oz sultanas

method

1 Cream the butter and sugar together in a mixing bowl. Blend in the egg, milk and vanilla and almond extracts until thoroughly combined. Chop the hazelnuts finely.

2 In a mixing bowl, sift the flour, allspice, bicarbonate of soda and salt together. Add to the creamed mixture slowly, stirring constantly. Mix in the oats, sultanas and hazelnuts.

3 Put 30 rounded tablespoonfuls of the mixture onto 2 large greased baking sheets, spaced well apart to allow for spreading. Transfer to a preheated oven, 190°C/375°F/Gas Mark 5, and bake for 12–15 minutes, or until the cookies are golden brown. Remove from the oven and place on a wire rack to cool before serving.

desserts

Desserts were originally 'created' to make full use of produce that was only available for a very short season, long before sophisticated preserving equipment, such as the refrigerator and freezer, was invented! As a result, fruits, nuts, eggs and dairy produce have been transformed into the most wonderful creations, becoming ever more elegant as their role changed from necessity to sheer pleasure.

Traditional fruit pies have evolved from a simple fruit filling encased in pastry, like the Forest Fruit Pie, to some glorious variations on the theme. Toffee Apple Tart, Pear & Pecan Strudel, Pear Tarte Tatin and Blackberry Tart with Cassis Cream are delicious examples of how to make the most of nature's bounty. An alternative way to use fruit is in Peach Cobbler, with a soft batter topping, or a classic dish from France, Cherry Clafoutis – the cherries float in a creamy batter scented with vanilla extract.

Nuts are also a superb ingredient for desserts. Try Florentine Praline Tartlets, Almond Tart, Sicilian Marzipan Tart with Candied Fruit, or an old favourite, Pecan Pie. And if you can't do without chocolate, there are recipes for Chocolate Nut Strudel, Mississippi Mud Pie, Chocolate Fudge Tart, Double Chocolate Roulade and that most unusual of baked desserts – Baked Chocolate Alaska. Heaven!

toffee apple tart

ingredients

SERVES 6

butter, for greasing
flour, for sprinkling
300 g/10 oz ready-made shortcrust pastry

filling

1.3 kg/3 lb sweet dessert apples, peeled and cored
1 tsp lemon juice
3 heaped tbsp butter
100 g/3½ oz caster sugar
200 g/7 oz granulated sugar
75 ml/2½ fl oz cold water
150 ml/5 fl oz double cream, plus extra for serving

method

1 Lightly grease a 22-cm/9-inch loose-based fluted tart tin. Roll out the pastry on a lightly floured work surface and line the tin with it, then roll the rolling pin over the tin to trim the excess dough. Fit a piece of baking paper into the tart case and fill with dried beans. Chill in the refrigerator for 30 minutes, then bake for 10 minutes in a preheated oven, 190°C/375°F/ Gas Mark 5. Remove the beans and paper and return to the oven for 5 minutes.

2 Meanwhile, take 4 apples, cut each one into 8 pieces and toss in the lemon juice. Melt the butter in a frying pan and sauté the apple pieces until just starting to caramelize and brown on the edges. Remove from the pan and set aside to cool.

3 Slice the remaining apples thinly, put them in a pan with the caster sugar and cook for about 20 minutes, until soft. Spoon into the pastry case and arrange the reserved apple pieces on top in a circle. Bake for 30 minutes.

4 Put the granulated sugar and water in a pan and heat until the sugar dissolves. Boil to form a caramel. Remove from the heat and add the cream, stirring constantly to combine into toffee. Remove the tart from the oven, pour the toffee over the apples and chill for 1 hour. Serve with double cream.

chocolate nut strudel

ingredients

SERVES 6

- 150 g/5$^{1}/_{2}$ oz unsalted butter, plus extra for greasing
- 225 g/8 oz mixed chopped nuts
- 115 g/4 oz plain chocolate, chopped
- 115 g/4 oz milk chocolate, chopped
- 115 g/4 oz white chocolate, chopped
- 200 g/7 oz filo pastry, thawed if frozen
- 3 tbsp golden syrup
- 55 g/2 oz icing sugar
- ice cream, to serve

method

1 Lightly grease a baking sheet with butter. Set aside 1 tablespoon of the nuts. Mix the 3 types of chocolate together.

2 Place 1 sheet of filo on a clean tea towel. Melt the butter and brush the sheet of filo with the butter, drizzle with a little syrup and sprinkle with some nuts and chocolate. Place another sheet of filo on top and repeat until you have used all the nuts and chocolate.

3 Use the tea towel to help you carefully roll up the strudel and place on the baking sheet, drizzle with a little more syrup and sprinkle with the reserved nuts. Bake in a preheated oven, 190°C/375°F/Gas Mark 5, for 20–25 minutes. If the nuts start to brown too much, cover the strudel with a sheet of foil.

4 Sprinkle the strudel with icing sugar, slice and eat warm with ice cream.

pear & pecan strudel

ingredients

SERVES 4

2 ripe pears
4 tbsp butter
55 g/2 oz fresh white breadcrumbs
55 g/2 oz shelled pecans, chopped
25 g/1 oz muscovado sugar
finely grated rind of 1 orange
100 g/3½ oz filo pastry, thawed if frozen
6 tbsp orange blossom honey
2 tbsp orange juice
sifted icing sugar, for dusting
strained plain yogurt, to serve (optional)

method

1 Peel, core and chop the pears. Melt 1 tablespoon of the butter in a frying pan and gently sauté the breadcrumbs until golden. Transfer the breadcrumbs to a bowl and add the pears, nuts, muscovado sugar and orange rind. Place the remaining butter in a small pan and heat until melted.

2 Set aside 1 sheet of filo pastry, keeping it well wrapped, and brush the remaining filo sheets with a little melted butter. Spoon a little of the nut filling onto 1 buttered filo sheet, leaving a 2.5-cm/1-inch margin around the edge. Build up the strudel by placing the remaining buttered filo sheets on top of the first, spreading each one with nut filling as you build up the layers. Drizzle the honey and orange juice over the top.

3 Fold the short ends over the filling, then roll up, starting at a long side. Carefully lift onto a baking sheet, with the join uppermost. Brush with any remaining melted butter and crumple the reserved sheet of filo pastry around the strudel. Bake in a preheated oven, 200°C/400°F/Gas Mark 6, for 25 minutes, or until golden and crisp. Dust with sifted icing sugar and serve warm with strained plain yogurt, if using.

pear tarte tatin

ingredients

SERVES 6

6 tbsp butter
115 g/4 oz caster sugar
6 pears, peeled, halved and cored
flour, for dusting
225 g/8 oz ready-made puff pastry
double cream, to serve (optional)

method

1 Melt the butter and sugar in an ovenproof frying pan over medium heat. Stir carefully for 5 minutes until it turns to a light caramel colour. Take care because it gets very hot.

2 Remove the pan from the heat, place on a heatproof surface and arrange the pears, cut side up, in the caramel. Place one half in the centre and surround it with the others.

3 On a lightly floured work surface, roll out the dough to a round, slightly larger than the frying pan, and place it on top of the pears. Tuck the edges down into the pan.

4 Bake near the top of a preheated oven, 200°C/400°F/ Gas Mark 6, for 20–25 minutes until the pastry is well risen and golden brown. Remove from the oven and cool for 2 minutes.

5 Invert the tart onto a serving dish that is larger than the frying pan and has enough depth to take any juices that may run out. Remember that this is very hot so use a pair of thick oven gloves. Serve warm, with double cream if using.

banoffee pie

ingredients

SERVES 4

filling

- 3 x 400 g/14 oz cans sweetened condensed milk
- 4 ripe bananas
- juice of 1/2 lemon
- 1 tsp vanilla extract
- 75 g/2 3/4 oz plain chocolate, grated
- 475 ml/16 fl oz double cream, whipped

biscuit base

- 85 g/3 oz butter, melted, plus extra for greasing
- 150 g/5 1/2 oz digestive biscuits, crushed into crumbs
- 25 g/1 oz shelled almonds, toasted and ground
- 25 g/1 oz shelled hazelnuts, toasted and ground

method

1 Place the unopened cans of milk in a large pan and add enough water to cover them. Bring to a boil, then reduce the heat and simmer for 2 hours, topping up the water level to keep the cans covered. Carefully lift out the hot cans from the pan and cool.

2 Place the butter in a bowl and add the crushed digestive biscuits and ground nuts. Mix together well, then press the mixture evenly into the base and side of a greased 23-cm/9-inch tart tin. Bake in a preheated oven, 180°C/350°F/Gas Mark 4, for 10–12 minutes, then remove from the oven and cool.

3 Peel and slice the bananas and place in a bowl. Squeeze over the juice from the lemon, add the vanilla extract and mix together. Spread the banana mixture over the biscuit base in the tin, then spoon over the contents of the cooled cans of condensed milk.

4 Sprinkle over 50 g/1 3/4 oz of the chocolate, then top with a layer of whipped cream. Sprinkle over the remaining grated chocolate and serve the pie at room temperature.

blackberry tart with cassis cream

ingredients

SERVES 6

pastry

350 g/12 oz plain flour

pinch of salt

175 g/6 oz unsalted butter

50 g/1 3/4 oz caster sugar

cold water

filling

750 g/1 lb 10 oz blackberries

6 tbsp golden caster sugar

1 tbsp cassis

5 tsp semolina

1 egg white

to serve

300 ml/10 fl oz double cream

1 tbsp cassis

fresh mint leaves

method

1 To make the pastry, sift the flour and salt into a large bowl and rub in the butter. Stir in the sugar and add enough cold water to bring the dough together, then wrap in clingfilm and chill for 30 minutes.

2 Meanwhile, rinse and pick over the blackberries, then put in a bowl with 4 tbsp of the sugar and the cassis, stirring to coat.

3 Roll out the dough to a large circle, handling carefully because it is quite a soft dough. Leave the edges ragged and place on a baking sheet. Sprinkle the dough with the semolina, leaving a good 6-cm/2 1/2-inch edge. Pile the fruit into the centre and brush the edges of the dough with the egg white. Fold in the edges of the dough to overlap and enclose the fruit, making sure to press together the dough in order to close any gaps. Brush with the remaining egg white, sprinkle with the remaining sugar and bake in a preheated oven, 200°C/400°F/ Gas Mark 6, for 25 minutes.

4 To serve, whip the cream until it starts to thicken and stir in the cassis. Serve the tart hot, straight from the oven, with a good spoonful of the cassis cream and decorated with mint leaves.

peach cobbler

ingredients

SERVES 4–6

filling

6 peaches, peeled and sliced

4 tbsp caster sugar

1/2 tbsp lemon juice

1 1/2 tsp cornflour

1/2 tsp almond or vanilla extract

vanilla or pecan ice cream, to serve

pie topping

175 g/6 oz plain flour

115 g/4 oz caster sugar

1 1/2 tsp baking powder

1/2 tsp salt

85 g/3 oz butter, diced

1 egg

5–6 tbsp milk

method

1 Place the peaches in a 23-cm/9-inch square ovenproof dish that is also suitable for serving. Add the sugar, lemon juice, cornflour and almond extract and toss together. Bake the peaches in a preheated oven, 220°C/425°F/ Gas Mark 7, for 20 minutes.

2 Meanwhile, to make the topping, sift the flour, all but 2 tablespoons of the sugar, the baking powder and salt into a bowl. Rub in the butter with the fingertips until the mixture resembles breadcrumbs. Mix the egg and 5 tablespoons of the milk in a jug, then mix into the dry ingredients with a fork until a soft, sticky dough forms. If the dough seems too dry, stir in the extra tablespoon of milk.

3 Reduce the oven temperature to 200°C/ 400°F/Gas Mark 6. Remove the peaches from the oven and drop spoonfuls of the topping over the surface, without smoothing. Sprinkle with the remaining sugar, return to the oven and bake for a further 15 minutes, or until the topping is golden brown and firm – the topping will spread as it cooks. Serve hot or at room temperature with ice cream.

cherry clafoutis

ingredients

SERVES 6

450 g/1 lb ripe fresh cherries, pitted
100 g/3½ oz caster sugar
2 large eggs
1 egg yolk
100 g/3½ oz plain flour
pinch of salt
175 ml/6 fl oz milk
4 tbsp double cream
1 tsp vanilla extract

method

1 Lightly grease a 1.25 litre/2½ pint ovenproof serving dish or a 25-cm/10-inch quiche dish. Scatter the cherries over the bottom of the prepared dish, then place the dish on a baking sheet.

2 Using an electric mixer, whisk the sugar, eggs and the egg yolk together until blended and a pale yellow colour, scraping down the sides of the bowl as necessary.

3 Beat in the flour and salt, then slowly beat in the milk, cream and vanilla extract until a light, smooth batter forms. Pour the batter into the dish.

4 Transfer the filled dish on the baking sheet to a preheated oven, 200°C/400°F/Gas Mark 6, and bake for 45 minutes, or until the top is golden brown and the batter is set.

5 Let the pudding stand for at least 5 minutes, then serve hot, or at room temperature.

new york cheesecake

ingredients

SERVES 8–10

6 tbsp butter

200 g/7 oz digestive biscuits, crushed

sunflower oil, for brushing

400 g/14 oz cream cheese

2 large eggs

140 g/5 oz caster sugar

1½ tsp vanilla extract

450 ml/16 fl oz soured cream

blueberry topping

55 g/2 oz caster sugar

4 tbsp water

250 g/9 oz fresh blueberries

1 tsp arrowroot

method

1 Melt the butter in a pan over low heat. Stir in the crushed biscuits, then spread in a 20-cm/8-inch springform tin brushed with oil. Place the cream cheese, eggs, 100 g/3½ oz of the sugar and ½ teaspoon of the vanilla extract in a food processor and process until smooth. Pour over the biscuit base and smooth the top. Place on a baking sheet and bake in a preheated oven, 190°C/375°F/Gas Mark 5, for 20 minutes until set. Remove from the oven and leave for 20 minutes. Leave the oven on.

2 Mix the cream with the remaining sugar and vanilla extract in a bowl. Spoon over the cheesecake. Return it to the oven for 10 minutes. Remove from the oven, cool, then chill in the refrigerator for 8 hours, or overnight.

3 To make the topping, place the sugar in a pan with 2 tablespoons of the water over low heat and stir until the sugar is dissolved. Increase the heat, add the blueberries, cover and cook for a few minutes, or until they begin to soften. Remove from the heat. Mix the arrowroot and remaining water in a bowl, add to the fruit and stir until smooth. Return to low heat. Cook until the juice thickens and turns translucent. Set aside to cool.

4 Remove the cheesecake from the tin 1 hour before serving. Spoon the fruit topping over and chill until ready to serve.

forest fruit pie

ingredients

SERVES 4

filling

225 g/8 oz blueberries
225 g/8 oz raspberries
225 g/8 oz blackberries
3 tbsp caster sugar
2 tbsp icing sugar, to decorate
whipped cream, to serve (optional)

pastry

225 g/8 oz plain flour, plus extra for dusting
25 g/1 oz ground hazelnuts
100 g/3½ oz butter, cut into small pieces, plus extra for greasing
55 g/2 oz caster sugar
finely grated rind of 1 lemon
1 egg yolk, beaten
4 tbsp milk

method

1 Place the fruit in a pan with the sugar and simmer gently, stirring frequently, for 5 minutes. Remove the pan from the heat.

2 Sift the flour into a bowl, then add the hazelnuts. Rub in the butter with the fingertips until the mixture resembles breadcrumbs, then sift in the sugar. Add the lemon rind, egg yolk and 3 tablespoons of the milk and mix. Turn out onto a lightly floured work surface and knead briefly. Wrap and chill in the refrigerator for 30 minutes.

3 Grease a 20-cm/8-inch pie dish with butter. Roll out two-thirds of the pastry to a thickness of 5 mm/¼ inch and use it to line the base and side of the dish. Spoon the fruit into the pastry case. Brush the rim with water, then roll out the remaining pastry to cover the pie. Trim and crimp round the edge, then make 2 small slits in the top and decorate with 2 leaf shapes cut out from the dough trimmings. Brush all over with the remaining milk. Bake in a preheated oven, 190°C/375°F/Gas Mark 5, for 40 minutes.

4 Remove the pie from the oven, sprinkle with the icing sugar and serve with whipped cream, if using.

mississippi mud pie

ingredients

SERVES 8

pastry

225 g/8 oz plain flour, plus extra for dusting
2 tbsp cocoa powder
150 g/5½ oz butter
2 tbsp caster sugar
1–2 tbsp cold water

filling

175 g/6 oz butter
350 g/12 oz brown sugar
4 eggs, lightly beaten
4 tbsp cocoa powder, sifted
150 g/5½ oz plain chocolate
300 ml/10 fl oz single cream
1 tsp chocolate extract

to decorate

425 ml/15 fl oz double cream, whipped
chocolate flakes and curls

method

1 To make the pastry, sift the flour and cocoa into a mixing bowl. Rub in the butter with the fingertips until the mixture resembles fine breadcrumbs. Stir in the sugar and enough cold water to mix to a soft dough. Wrap the dough and chill in the refrigerator for 15 minutes.

2 Roll out the dough on a lightly floured work surface and use to line a 23-cm/9-inch loose-based tart tin or ceramic pie dish. Line with baking paper and fill with dried beans. Bake in a preheated oven, 190°C/375°F/Gas Mark 5, for 15 minutes. Remove from the oven and take out the paper and beans. Bake the pastry case for a further 10 minutes.

3 To make the filling, beat the butter and sugar together in a bowl and gradually beat in the eggs with the cocoa. Melt the chocolate and beat it into the mixture with the single cream and the chocolate extract.

4 Reduce the oven temperature to 160°C/325°F/Gas Mark 3. Pour the mixture into the pastry case and bake for 45 minutes, or until the filling has set gently.

5 Cool the mud pie completely, then transfer it to a serving plate, if you like. Cover with the whipped cream. Decorate the pie with chocolate flakes and curls and then chill until ready to serve.

florentine praline tartlets

ingredients

SERVES 6

praline

100 g/3½ oz granulated sugar
3 tbsp water
50 g/1¾ oz slivered almonds
butter

pastry

125 g/4½ oz plain flour
pinch of salt
75 g/2½ oz cold butter, cut into pieces
1 tsp icing sugar
cold water

frangipane

75 g/2½ oz butter
2 eggs
75 g/2½ oz caster sugar
2 tbsp plain flour
115 g/4 oz ground almonds

topping

8 natural candied cherries, chopped
2 tbsp mixed candied peel, chopped
100 g/3½ oz plain chocolate, chopped

method

1 To make the praline, put the sugar and water in a pan and dissolve the sugar over low heat. Do not stir the sugar, just let it boil for 10 minutes, until it turns to caramel, then stir in the nuts and turn out onto buttered foil. Set aside to cool and harden. When cold break up the praline and chop into smallish pieces.

2 Grease 6 x 9-cm/3½-inch loose-based fluted tart tins. Sift the flour and salt into a food processor, add the butter and process until the mixture resembles fine breadcrumbs. Add the sugar and a little cold water and pulse to bring the dough together. Turn out onto a floured work surface and divide into 6 pieces. Roll out each piece and use to line the tart tins. Roll the rolling pin over the tins to trim the excess dough. Freeze for 30 minutes.

3 Meanwhile, make the frangipane. Melt the butter and beat the eggs and sugar together. Stir the melted butter into the egg and sugar mixture, then add the flour and almonds.

4 Bake the tart cases blind, straight from the freezer, for 10 minutes in a preheated oven, 200°C/400°F/Gas Mark 6. Divide the frangipane between the tart cases and return to the oven for 8–10 minutes. Meanwhile, mix the cherries, peel, chocolate and praline together. Divide between the tarts while they are still hot so that some of the chocolate melts. Serve cold.

chocolate fudge tart

ingredients

SERVES 6

flour, for sprinkling
350 g/12 oz ready-made shortcrust pastry
icing sugar, for dusting

filling

140 g/5 oz plain chocolate, finely chopped
175 g/6 oz butter, diced
350 g/12 oz golden granulated sugar
100 g/3½ oz plain flour
½ tsp vanilla extract
6 eggs, beaten

to decorate

150 ml/5 fl oz whipped cream
ground cinnamon

method

1 Roll out the pastry on a lightly floured work surface and use to line a 20-cm/8-inch deep loose-based tart tin. Prick the dough base lightly with a fork, then line with foil and fill with dried beans. Bake in a preheated oven, 200°C/400°F/Gas Mark 6, for 12–15 minutes, or until the dough no longer looks raw. Remove the beans and foil and bake for a further 10 minutes, or until the dough is firm. Set aside to cool. Reduce the oven temperature to 180°C/350°F/Gas Mark 4.

2 To make the filling, place the chocolate and butter in a heatproof bowl and set over a pan of gently simmering water until melted. Stir until smooth, then remove from the heat and cool. Place the sugar, flour, vanilla extract and eggs in a separate bowl and whisk until well blended. Stir in the butter and chocolate mixture.

3 Pour the filling into the pastry case and bake in the oven for 50 minutes, or until the filling is just set. Transfer to a wire rack to cool completely. Dust with icing sugar before serving with whipped cream sprinkled lightly with cinnamon.

almond tart

ingredients

SERVES 8

280 g/10 oz plain flour, plus extra for dusting
150 g/5½ oz caster sugar
1 tsp finely grated lemon rind
pinch of salt
150 g/5½ oz unsalted butter, chilled and cut into small dice
1 medium egg, beaten lightly
1 tbsp chilled water

175 g/6 oz unsalted butter, at room temperature
175 g/6 oz caster sugar
3 large eggs
175 g/6 oz finely ground almonds
2 tsp plain flour
1 tbsp finely grated orange rind
½ tsp almond extract
icing sugar, to decorate
soured cream (optional), to serve

method

1 To make the pastry, put the flour, sugar, lemon rind and salt in a bowl. Rub or cut in the butter until the mixture resembles fine breadcrumbs. Combine the egg and water, then slowly pour into the flour, stirring with a fork until a coarse mass forms. Shape into a ball and chill for at least 1 hour.

2 Roll out the pastry on a lightly floured work surface until 3 mm/⅛ inch thick. Use to line a greased 25-cm/10-inch tart tin. Return to the refrigerator for 15 minutes, then cover the pastry case with foil and fill with dried beans. Place in a preheated oven, 220°C/425°F/Gas Mark 7 and bake for 12 minutes. Remove the dried beans and foil and return the pastry case to the oven for 4 minutes. Remove from the oven and reduce the oven temperature to 200°C/400°F/Gas Mark 6.

3 Meanwhile, make the filling. Beat the butter and sugar until creamy. Beat in the eggs, 1 at a time. Add the almonds, flour, orange rind and almond extract and beat until blended.

4 Spoon the filling into the pastry case and smooth the surface. Bake for 30–35 minutes until the top is golden and the tip of a knife inserted in the centre comes out clean. Cool completely on a wire rack, then dust with sifted icing sugar. Serve with a spoonful of soured cream, if using.

sicilian marzipan tart with candied fruit

ingredients

SERVES 6

pastry

- 125 g/4½ oz plain flour, plus extra for dusting
- pinch of salt
- 75 g/2½ oz cold butter, cut into pieces
- cold water

filling

- 300 g/10½ oz marzipan
- 175 g/6 oz ground almonds
- 150 g/5½ oz unsalted butter
- 100 g/3½ oz caster sugar
- 55 g/2 oz plain flour
- 2 eggs
- 55 g/2 oz sultanas
- 55 g/2 oz mixed candied peel, chopped
- 55 g/2 oz natural candied cherries, halved
- 55 g/2 oz flaked almonds

method

1 Lightly grease a 22-cm/9-inch loose-based fluted tart tin. Sift the flour and salt into a food processor, add the butter and process until the mixture resembles fine breadcrumbs. Add just enough cold water to bring the dough together. Turn out onto a work surface dusted with more flour and roll out the dough 8 cm/3¼ inches larger than the tin. Lift the dough into the tin and press to fit. Roll the rolling pin over the tin to trim the excess dough. Fit a piece of baking paper into the tart case and fill with dried beans.

2 Chill for 30 minutes, then bake for 10 minutes in a preheated oven, 190°C/375°F/Gas Mark 5. Remove the beans and paper and bake for a further 5 minutes. Lower the temperature to 180°C/350°F/Gas Mark 4. Grate the marzipan straight onto the base of the warm pastry.

3 Put the ground almonds, butter and sugar in a food processor and pulse until smooth. Add 1 tbsp flour and 1 of the eggs and blend, then add another 1 tbsp flour and the other egg and blend. Finally add the remaining flour. Scoop the mixture into a bowl and stir in the sultanas, peel and cherries. Spoon the mixture over the marzipan, sprinkle with the flaked almonds and bake for 40 minutes. Serve cold.

caramelized lemon tart

ingredients

SERVES 6

pastry

200 g/7 oz plain flour, plus extra for dusting
pinch of salt
100 g/3½ oz cold butter, cut into pieces
2 tbsp caster sugar
1 egg yolk
cold water

filling

5 lemons
2 eggs
275 g/10 oz caster sugar
175 g/6 oz ground almonds
100 ml/3½ fl oz water
125 ml/4 fl oz whipping cream, plus extra for serving

method

1 Lightly grease a 22-cm/9-inch loose-based fluted tart tin. Sift the flour and salt into a food processor, add the butter and process until the mixture resembles fine breadcrumbs. Add the sugar and egg yolk and just enough cold water to bring the dough together. Roll out the dough on a lightly floured work surface to a circle 8 cm/3¼ inches larger than the tin. Lift the dough carefully into the tin, press to fit and trim the excess dough. Fit baking paper into the tart case and fill with dried beans. Chill for 30 minutes, then bake blind for 10 minutes in a preheated oven, 190°C/375°F/Gas Mark 5. Remove the beans and paper and bake for 5 minutes more.

2 Put the juice and finely grated rind of 3 of the lemons in a bowl. Add the eggs, 85 g/3 oz of the sugar, the ground almonds and the cream, whisking to combine. Pour into the pastry case and bake for 25 minutes.

3 Thinly slice the remaining 2 lemons, discarding the seeds and ends. Heat the remaining sugar and water in a pan until the sugar is dissolved. Simmer for 5 minutes, then add the lemon slices and boil for 10 minutes. Arrange the lemon slices over the surface of the cooked tart in a spiral pattern. Drizzle over the lemon syrup. Serve warm or cold, with whipped cream.

truffled honey tart

ingredients

SERVES 6

pastry

125 g/4½ oz plain flour, plus extra for dusting
pinch of salt
75 g/2½ oz cold butter, cut into pieces
1 tsp icing sugar
cold water

filling

225 g/8 oz curd cheese
115 g/4 oz cream cheese
125 ml/4 fl oz double cream
2 egg yolks, plus 1 whole egg
2 tbsp caster sugar
4 tbsp flower honey, plus extra for drizzling
crystallized violets or sugared rose petals, to decorate

method

1 Lightly grease a 22-cm/9-inch loose-based fluted tart tin. Sift the flour and salt into a food processor, add the butter and process until the mixture resembles fine breadcrumbs. Add the sugar and a little cold water, just enough to bring the dough together. Turn out onto a work surface dusted with more flour and roll out the dough 8 cm/3¼ inches larger than the tin. Carefully lift the dough into the tin and press to fit. Roll the rolling pin over the tin to trim the excess dough. Fit a piece of baking paper into the tart case, fill with dried beans and chill in the refrigerator for 30 minutes.

2 Remove the pastry case from the refrigerator and bake blind for 10 minutes in a preheated oven, 190°C/375°F/Gas Mark 5, then remove the beans and paper and bake for a further 5 minutes.

3 Mix the curd cheese, cream cheese and cream together until smooth, then stir in the egg yolks and whole egg plus the sugar and honey until completely smooth. Pour into the pastry case and bake for 30 minutes. Remove from the oven and cool in the tin for 10 minutes. Drizzle with more honey and decorate with violets or petals.

baked chocolate alaska

ingredients

SERVES 4

butter, for greasing
2 eggs
175 g/6 oz caster sugar, plus 4 tbsp
4 tbsp plain flour
2 tbsp cocoa powder
3 egg whites
1 litre/1¾ pints good-quality chocolate ice cream

method

1 Grease an 18-cm/7-inch round cake tin and line the base with baking paper.

2 Whisk the eggs and the 4 tablespoons of sugar in a mixing bowl until very thick and pale. Sift the flour and cocoa together and carefully fold in.

3 Pour into the prepared tin and bake in a preheated oven, 220°C/425°F/Gas Mark 7, for 7 minutes, or until springy to the touch. Turn out and transfer to a wire rack to cool completely.

4 Whisk the egg whites in a clean, greasefree bowl until soft peaks form. Gradually add the remaining sugar, whisking until you have a thick, glossy meringue. Place the sponge on a baking sheet. Soften the ice cream in the refrigerator and pile it onto the centre to form a dome.

5 Pipe or spread the meringue over the ice cream, making sure it is completely enclosed. (At this point the dessert can be frozen, if wished.) Return to the oven for 5 minutes, until the meringue is a light golden brown. Serve at once.

mixed fruit pavlova

ingredients

SERVES 4

6 egg whites
pinch of cream of tartar
pinch of salt
300 g/10 oz caster sugar
600 ml/20 fl oz double cream
1 tsp vanilla extract
2 kiwi fruits, peeled and sliced
250 g/9 oz strawberries, hulled and sliced
3 ripe peaches, sliced
1 ripe mango, peeled and sliced
2 tbsp orange liqueur, such as Cointreau
fresh mint leaves, to decorate

method

1 Line 3 baking sheets with baking paper, then draw a 22-cm/8½-inch circle in the centre of each one. Beat the egg whites into stiff peaks. Mix in the cream of tartar and salt. Gradually add 200 g/7 oz of sugar. Beat for 2 minutes until glossy. Fill a piping bag with the mixture and use it to fill each circle, making them slightly domed in the centre. Bake in a preheated oven, 110°C/225°F/Gas Mark ¼, for 3 hours. Remove from the oven and cool.

2 Whip together the cream and vanilla extract with all but 2 tablespoons of the remaining sugar. Put the fruit into a separate bowl and stir in the liqueur.

3 Put one meringue circle onto a serving plate, then spread over one-third of the sugared cream. Spread over one-third of the fruit, then top with a meringue. Spread over another third of the cream, then another third of the fruit. Top with the last meringue. Spread over the remaining cream, followed by the remaining fruit. Decorate with mint leaves and serve.

pecan pie

ingredients

SERVES 8

pastry

250 g/9 oz plain flour
pinch of salt
115 g/4 oz butter, cut into small pieces
1 tbsp lard or vegetable shortening, cut into small pieces
55 g/2 oz golden caster sugar
6 tbsp cold milk

filling

3 eggs
250 g/8 oz muscovado sugar
1 tsp vanilla extract
pinch of salt
85 g/3 oz butter, melted
3 tbsp golden syrup
3 tbsp treacle
350 g/12 oz shelled pecans, roughly chopped
pecan halves, to decorate
whipped cream or vanilla ice cream, to serve

method

1 To make the pastry, sift the flour and salt into a mixing bowl and rub in the butter and lard with the fingertips until the mixture resembles fine breadcrumbs. Work in the caster sugar and add the milk. Work the mixture into a soft dough. Wrap the dough in cling film and chill in the refrigerator for 30 minutes.

2 Roll out the pastry and use it to line a 23–25-cm/9–10 inch tart tin. Trim off the excess by running the rolling pin over the top of the tart tin. Line with baking paper and fill with dried beans. Bake in a preheated oven, 200°C/400°F/Gas Mark 6, for 20 minutes. Take out of the oven and remove the paper and dried beans. Reduce the oven temperature to 180°C/350°F/Gas Mark 4. Place a baking sheet in the oven.

3 To make the filling, place the eggs in a bowl and beat lightly. Beat in the muscovado sugar, vanilla extract and salt. Stir in the butter, syrup, treacle and chopped nuts. Pour into the pastry case and decorate with the pecan halves.

4 Place on the heated baking sheet and bake in the oven for 35-40 minutes until the filling is set. Serve warm or at room temperature with whipped cream or vanilla ice cream.

lemon meringue pie

ingredients

SERVES 8–10

butter, for greasing
plain flour, for dusting
250 g/9 oz ready-made shortcrust pastry, thawed if frozen
3 tbsp cornflour
85 g/3 oz caster sugar
grated rind of 3 lemons
300 ml/10 fl oz cold water
150 ml/5 fl oz lemon juice
3 egg yolks
55 g/2 oz unsalted butter, cut into small cubes

meringue

3 egg whites
175 g/6 oz caster sugar
1 tsp golden granulated sugar

method

1 Grease a 25-cm/10-inch fluted tart tin. On a lightly floured work surface, roll out the pastry and ease it into the tin, rolling off the excess. Prick the bottom of the tart case and chill, uncovered, for 30 minutes. Line with baking paper and fill with dried beans. Bake on a preheated baking sheet in a preheated oven, 200°C/400°F/Gas Mark 6, for 15 minutes. Remove the beans and paper and return to the oven for 10 minutes. Remove and reduce the temperature to 150°C/300°F/Gas Mark 2.

2 Put the cornflour, sugar and lemon rind into a pan. Blend in a little of the water to make a smooth paste. Gradually add the remaining water and the lemon juice. Bring to a boil over medium heat, stirring continuously. Simmer gently for 1 minute until smooth and glossy. Remove from the heat. Beat in the egg yolks, 1 at a time, then the butter. Place the pan in a bowl of cold water to cool the filling, then spoon it into the tart case.

3 To make the meringue, whisk the egg whites until thick and in soft peaks. Gradually add the caster sugar, whisking well with each addition. Spoon the meringue over the filling to cover it completely. Swirl the meringue into peaks and sprinkle with granulated sugar. Bake for 20–30 minutes until the meringue is crispy and pale gold (the centre should still be soft). Cool slightly before serving.

cappuccino soufflés

ingredients

SERVES 6

- 6 tbsp whipping cream
- 2 tsp instant espresso coffee granules
- 2 tbsp Kahlua
- butter, for greasing
- 3 large eggs, separated, plus 1 extra egg white
- 2 tbsp golden caster sugar, plus extra for coating
- 150 g/5½ oz plain chocolate, melted and cooled
- cocoa powder, for dusting
- vanilla ice cream and chocolate biscuits, to serve

method

1 Place the cream in a small, heavy-based pan and heat gently. Stir in the coffee until it has dissolved, then stir in the Kahlua. Divide the coffee mixture between 6 lightly greased 175-ml/6 fl oz ramekins coated with caster sugar.

2 Place the egg whites in a clean, greasefree bowl and whisk until soft peaks form, then gradually whisk in the sugar until stiff but not dry. Stir the egg yolks and melted chocolate together in a separate bowl, then stir in a little of the whisked egg whites. Gradually fold in the remaining egg whites.

3 Divide the mixture between the ramekins. Place the ramekins on a baking sheet and bake in a preheated oven, 190°C/375°F/Gas Mark 5, for 15 minutes, or until just set. Dust with cocoa powder and serve immediately with vanilla ice cream and chocolate biscuits.

double chocolate roulade

ingredients

SERVES 8

4 eggs, separated
115 g/4 oz golden caster sugar
115 g/4 oz plain chocolate, melted and cooled
1 tsp instant coffee granules, dissolved in 2 tbsp hot water, cooled
icing sugar, to decorate
cocoa powder, for dusting
fresh raspberries, to serve

filling

250 ml/9 fl oz whipping cream
140 g/5 oz white chocolate, broken into pieces
3 tbsp Tia Maria

method

1 Line a 23 x 33-cm/9 x 13-inch Swiss roll tin with nonstick baking paper. Whisk the egg yolks and sugar in a bowl until pale and mousse-like. Fold in the chocolate, then the coffee. Place the egg whites in a clean bowl and whisk until stiff but not dry. Stir a little of the egg whites into the chocolate mixture, then fold in the remainder. Pour into the tin and bake in a preheated oven, 180°C/350°F/ Gas Mark 4, for 15–20 minutes, or until firm. Cover with a damp tea towel and let stand in the tin for 8 hours, or overnight.

2 Meanwhile, make the filling. Heat the cream until almost boiling. Place the chocolate in a food processor and chop coarsely. With the motor running, pour the cream through the feed tube. Process until smooth. Stir in the Tia Maria. Transfer to a bowl and cool. Chill for 8 hours, or overnight.

3 To assemble the roulade, whip the chocolate cream until soft peaks form. Cut a sheet of waxed paper larger than the roulade, place on a work surface and sift icing sugar over it. Turn the roulade out onto the paper. Peel away the lining paper. Spread the chocolate cream over the roulade and roll up from the short side nearest to you. Transfer to a dish, seam-side down. Chill for 2 hours, then dust with cocoa. Serve with raspberries.

baking with yeast

Baking with yeast seems to hold terrors for those who have never tried it, and yet it is really easy, especially now that easy-blend dried yeast has largely superseded the use of fresh yeast. Yeast cooking needs a little planning because of the time required for the dough to rise, but there is absolutely nothing to beat the aroma of fresh bread wafting through your home, so the wait is more than worth it.

Sweet breads are delicious for breakfast or brunch, or with coffee or tea at any time of day. Life will never be the same once you've mastered those flaky, buttery French specialities, Croissants and Pains au Chocolat, or the slightly less messy-to-eat brioche – we've selected a delicious Orange & Raisin Brioche for you to try. Cinnamon Swirls and Crown Loaf are fun to eat, too – you can bite into them tidily, or unroll them to pull out the fruity bits of filling!

Savoury breads are the perfect accompaniment to soups, salads, and main meals. Both sweet and savoury breads are great for making sandwiches – try Apricot & Walnut Bread with a filling of cream cheese, or Olive & Sun-dried Tomato Bread packed with your favourite cold cuts and some watercress. And if you love pizza, there's a recipe for a basic Cheese & Tomato Pizza – you can dress it up all you like.

fresh croissants

ingredients

SERVES 12

500 g/1 lb 2 oz white bread flour, plus extra for dusting
40 g/1½ oz caster sugar
1 tsp salt
2 tsp easy-blend dried yeast
300 ml/10 fl oz milk, heated until just warm to the touch
300 g/10½ oz butter, softened, flattened with a rolling pin between 2 sheets of greaseproof paper to form a rectangle 5 mm/¼ inch thick, then chilled in the refrigerator, plus extra for greasing
1 egg, lightly beaten with 1 tbsp milk, to glaze
jam, to serve (optional)

you will need

a cardboard triangular template, base 18 cm/7 inches and sides 20 cm/8 inches

method

1 Stir the dry ingredients in a large bowl, make a well in the centre and add the milk. Mix to a soft dough, adding more milk if too dry. Knead on a lightly floured work surface for 5–10 minutes, or until smooth and elastic. Let rise in a large, greased bowl, covered, in a warm place until doubled in size.

2 Knead the dough for 1 minute. Let the butter soften slightly. Roll out the dough on a well-floured work surface to 46 x 15 cms/18 x 6 inches. Place the butter in the centre. Then with the short end of the dough towards you, fold the top third down towards the centre, then fold the bottom third up and squeeze the edges together gently. Rotate so that the fold is to your left and the top flap towards your right. Roll out to a rectangle and fold again. If the butter feels soft, wrap the dough in clingfilm and chill. Repeat the rolling process twice more. Cut the dough in half. Roll out one half into a triangle 5 mm/¼ inch thick (keep the other half refrigerated). Use the cardboard template to cut out the croissants.

3 Brush the triangles lightly with the glaze. Roll into croissant shapes, starting at the base and tucking under the point. Brush again with the glaze and place on an ungreased baking sheet. Let double in size, then bake in a preheated oven, 200°C/400°F/Gas Mark 6, for 15–20 minutes until golden. Serve with jam, if liked.

orange & raisin brioches

ingredients

SERVES 12

55 g/2 oz butter, melted, plus extra for greasing
225 g/8 oz strong white bread flour, plus extra for dusting
$^1/_2$ tsp salt
2 tsp easy-blend dried yeast
1 tbsp golden caster sugar
55 g/2 oz raisins
grated rind of 1 orange
2 tbsp tepid water
2 eggs, beaten
vegetable oil, for brushing
1 beaten egg, for glazing
butter, to serve (optional)

method

1 Grease 12 individual brioche moulds. Sift the flour and salt into a warmed bowl and stir in the yeast, sugar, raisins and orange rind. Make a well in the centre. In a separate bowl, mix together the water, eggs and melted butter and pour into the dry ingredients. Beat vigorously to make a soft dough. Turn out onto a lightly floured work surface and knead for 5 minutes, or until smooth and elastic. Brush a clean bowl with oil. Place the dough in the bowl, cover with clingfilm and let stand in a warm place for 1 hour, or until doubled in size.

2 Turn out onto a floured work surface, knead lightly for 1 minute, then roll into a rope shape. Cut into 12 equal pieces. Shape three-quarters of each piece into a ball and place in the prepared moulds. With a floured finger, press a hole in the centre of each. Shape the remaining pieces of dough into little plugs and press into the holes, flattening the top slightly.

3 Place the moulds on a baking sheet, cover lightly with oiled clingfilm and let stand in a warm place for 1 hour, until the dough comes almost to the top.

4 Brush the brioches with beaten egg and bake in a preheated oven, 220°C/425°F/Gas Mark 7, for 15 minutes, or until golden brown. Serve warm with butter, if you like.

pains au chocolat

ingredients

SERVES 8

100 g/3½ oz butter, plus extra for greasing

250 g/9 oz white bread flour, plus extra for dusting

1 tsp salt

2 tsp easy-blend dried yeast

175 ml/6 fl oz milk

2 tbsp golden caster sugar

1 tbsp oil, plus extra for brushing

115 g/4 oz plain chocolate, coarsely chopped

glaze

1 egg yolk

2 tbsp milk

method

1 Grease a baking sheet. Sift the flour and salt into a bowl and stir in the yeast. Make a well in the centre. Heat the milk in a pan until tepid. Add the sugar and oil and stir until the sugar has dissolved. Stir into the flour and mix well. Turn the dough out onto a lightly floured work surface and knead until smooth, then place in an oiled bowl. Cover and let rise in a warm place for 2–3 hours, or until doubled in size.

2 Knead on a floured work surface and roll into a rectangle 3 times as long as it is wide. Divide the butter into thirds. Dot one portion over the top two-thirds of the dough, leaving a 1-cm/ ½-inch margin round the edges. Fold the lower third up and the top third down. Seal the edges. Give the dough a half-turn. Roll into a rectangle. Repeat the process twice, then fold in half. Put into an oiled plastic bag. Chill for 1 hour.

3 Cut the dough in half and roll out into 2 rectangles of 30 x 15 cm/12 x 6 inches. Cut each half into 4 rectangles of 15 x 7.5 cm/ 6 x 3 inches. Sprinkle chocolate along one short end of each and roll up. Place on the baking sheet in a warm place for 2–3 hours, or until doubled in size. To glaze, mix the egg yolk and milk and brush over the rolls. Bake in a preheated oven, 220°C/425°F/Gas Mark 7, for 15–20 minutes, or until golden and well risen.

chocolate bread

ingredients

MAKES 1 LOAF

butter, for greasing
450 g/1 lb strong white bread flour, plus extra for dusting
25 g/1 oz cocoa powder
1 tsp salt
1 sachet easy-blend dried yeast
2 tbsp brown sugar
1 tbsp corn oil
300 ml/10 fl oz lukewarm water
butter, to serve

method

1 Lightly grease a 900-g/2-lb loaf tin with a little butter. Sift the flour and cocoa into a large bowl. Stir in the salt, yeast and brown sugar. Pour in the oil and water and mix together to form a dough.

2 Knead the dough on a lightly floured work surface for 5 minutes. Alternatively, use an electric mixer with a dough hook. Place the dough in a greased bowl, cover and let rise in a warm place for 1 hour, or until doubled in size.

3 Punch down the dough and shape it into a loaf. Place the dough in the tin, cover and let stand in a warm place for a further 30 minutes.

4 Bake the bread in a preheated oven, 200°C/400°F/Gas Mark 6, for 25–30 minutes, or until a hollow sound is heard when the bottom of the bread is tapped. Transfer the bread to a wire rack and cool completely. Cut into slices and serve with butter.

citrus bread

ingredients

MAKES 1 LOAF

- 4 tbsp butter, diced, plus extra for greasing
- 450 g/1 lb strong white bread flour, plus extra for dusting
- 1/2 tsp salt
- 50 g/1 3/4 oz caster sugar
- 1 sachet easy-blend dried yeast
- 5–6 tbsp orange juice
- 4 tbsp lemon juice
- 3–4 tbsp lime juice
- 150 ml/5 fl oz lukewarm water
- 1 orange
- 1 lemon
- 1 lime
- 2 tbsp honey, for glazing

method

1 Lightly grease a baking sheet with butter.

2 Sift the flour and salt into a large mixing bowl. Stir in the sugar and dried yeast. Rub in the butter with your fingertips until the mixture resembles breadcrumbs. Add all of the fruit juices and the water and bring together with your fingers to form a dough.

3 Place the dough on a lightly floured work surface and knead for 5 minutes. Alternatively, use an electric mixer with a dough hook. Place the dough in a greased bowl, cover and let rise in a warm place for 1 hour, until doubled in size.

4 Meanwhile, grate the rind of the orange, lemon and lime. Knead the fruit rinds into the dough.

5 Divide the dough into 2 balls, making one slightly bigger than the other. Place the larger ball on the baking sheet and set the smaller one on top. Push a floured finger through the centre of the dough. Cover and let rise for about 40 minutes, or until springy to the touch.

6 Bake in a preheated oven, 220°C/425°F/Gas Mark 7, for 35 minutes. Remove from the oven and transfer to a wire rack. Glaze with the honey and cool completely.

stollen

ingredients

SERVES 10

85 g/3 oz currants
55 g/2 oz raisins
2 tbsp chopped candied peel
55 g/2 oz candied cherries, rinsed, dried and quartered
2 tbsp rum
55 g/2 oz butter
175 ml/6 fl oz milk
2 tbsp golden caster sugar
375 g/13 oz strong white bread flour, plus extra for dusting
1/2 tsp ground nutmeg
1/2 tsp ground cinnamon
seeds from 3 cardamoms
2 tsp easy-blend dried yeast
finely grated rind of 1 lemon
1 egg, beaten
40 g/1 1/2 oz flaked almonds
vegetable oil, for brushing
175 g/6 oz marzipan
melted butter, for brushing
sifted icing sugar, for dredging

method

1 Place the currants, raisins, peel and cherries in a bowl, stir in the rum and set aside. Place the butter, milk and sugar in a pan over low heat and stir until the sugar dissolves and the butter melts. Cool until lukewarm. Sift the flour, nutmeg and cinnamon into a bowl. Crush the cardamom seeds and add them. Stir in the yeast. Make a well in the centre, stir in the milk mixture, lemon rind and egg and beat into a dough.

2 Turn the dough out onto a floured work surface and knead for 5 minutes. Knead in the soaked fruit and the almonds. Transfer to a clean, oiled bowl. Cover with clingfilm and let stand in a warm place for up to 3 hours, or until doubled in size. Turn out onto a floured work surface, knead for 1–2 minutes, then roll out to a 25-cm/ 10-inch square.

3 Roll the marzipan into a sausage shorter than the length of the dough. Place in the centre. Fold the dough over the marzipan, overlapping it. Seal the ends. Place seam-side down on a greased baking sheet, cover with oiled clingfilm and let stand in a warm place for up to 2 hours, or until doubled in size. Preheat the oven to 190°C/375°F/Gas Mark 5. Bake for 40 minutes, or until golden and hollow sounding when tapped. Brush with melted butter, dredge with icing sugar and cool on a wire rack.

cinnamon swirls

ingredients

SERVES 12

2 tbsp butter, cut into small pieces, plus extra for greasing
225 g/8 oz strong white bread flour
1/2 tsp salt
1 sachet easy-blend dried yeast
1 egg, beaten
125 ml/4 fl oz warm milk
2 tbsp maple syrup

filling

4 tbsp butter, softened
2 tsp ground cinnamon
50 g/1 3/4 oz brown sugar
50 g/1 3/4 oz currants

method

1 Grease a 23-cm/9-inch square cake tin. Sift the flour and salt into a bowl. Stir in the yeast. Rub in the butter with your fingertips until the mixture resembles fine breadcrumbs. Add the egg and milk and mix to form a dough. Place in a greased bowl, cover and let stand in a warm place for 40 minutes, or until doubled in size.

2 Knead the dough lightly for 1 minute to punch it down, then roll out on a lightly floured work surface to form a rectangle measuring 30 x 23 cm/12 x 9 inches.

3 To make the filling, beat the butter, cinnamon and brown sugar together until the mixture is light and fluffy. Spread the filling over the dough, leaving a 2.5-cm/1-inch border all round. Sprinkle over the currants.

4 Carefully roll up the dough like a Swiss roll, starting at a long edge, and press down to seal. Using a sharp knife, cut the roll into 12 slices. Place them in the prepared tin, cover and let stand for 30 minutes.

5 Bake the swirls in a preheated oven, 190°C/375°F/Gas Mark 5, for 20–30 minutes, or until well risen. Brush the swirls with the syrup and cool slightly before serving warm.

crown loaf

ingredients

MAKES 1 LOAF

2 tbsp butter, diced, plus extra for greasing
225 g/8 oz strong white bread flour, plus extra for dusting
1/2 tsp salt
1 sachet easy-blend dried yeast
125 ml/4 fl oz lukewarm milk
1 egg, beaten lightly

filling

4 tbsp butter, softened
50 g/1 3/4 oz brown sugar
2 tbsp chopped hazelnuts
1 tbsp chopped preserved ginger
50 g/1 3/4 oz candied peel
1 tbsp rum or brandy

icing

100 g/3 1/2 oz icing sugar
2 tbsp lemon juice

method

1 Grease a baking sheet with a little butter. Sift the flour and salt into a large mixing bowl. Stir in the yeast. Rub in the butter with your fingertips. Add the milk and egg and bring together with your fingers to form a dough.

2 Place the dough in a greased bowl, cover and let stand in a warm place for about 40 minutes, until doubled in size. Punch down the dough lightly for 1 minute, then roll out into a rectangle measuring 30 x 23 cm/ 12 x 9 inches.

3 To make the filling, cream the butter and sugar together in a large bowl until light and fluffy. Stir in the hazelnuts, ginger, candied peel and rum or brandy. Spread the filling over the dough, leaving a 2.5-cm/1-inch border around the edges.

4 Roll up the dough, starting from one of the long edges, into a sausage shape. Cut into slices at 5-cm/2-inch intervals and place the slices in a circle on the baking sheet, sides just touching. Cover and stand in a warm place to rise for 30 minutes.

5 Bake in a preheated oven, 190°C/375°F/Gas Mark 5, for 20–30 minutes or until golden. Meanwhile, mix the icing sugar with enough lemon juice to form a thin icing. Cool the loaf slightly before drizzling with icing. Allow the icing to set slightly before serving.

date & honey loaf

ingredients

SERVES 10

butter, for greasing
250 g/9 oz strong white bread flour, plus extra for dusting
75 g/2¾ oz strong brown bread flour
½ tsp salt
1 sachet easy-blend dried yeast
200 ml/7 fl oz lukewarm water
3 tbsp corn oil
3 tbsp honey
75 g/2¾ oz dried dates, chopped
2 tbsp sesame seeds

method

1 Grease a 900-g/2-lb loaf tin with butter. Sift the white and brown flours into a large bowl and stir in the salt and yeast. Pour in the water, oil and honey and mix to form a dough.

2 Place the dough on a lightly floured work surface and knead for 5 minutes, or until smooth, then place in a greased bowl. Cover and let rise in a warm place for 1 hour, or until doubled in size.

3 Knead in the dates and the sesame seeds. Shape the dough and place in the prepared loaf tin. Cover and let stand in a warm place for a further 30 minutes, or until springy to the touch.

4 Bake the loaf in a preheated oven, 220°C/425°F/Gas Mark 7, for 30 minutes, or until the bottom of the loaf sounds hollow when tapped. Transfer to a wire rack and cool completely. Serve cut into thick slices.

banana & orange bread

ingredients

MAKES 1 MEDIUM LOAF

500 g/1 lb 2 oz white bread flour, plus an extra 1–2 tbsp for sticky dough
1 tsp salt
1 tsp easy-blend dried yeast
3 tbsp butter, diced
2 medium ripe bananas or 1 large ripe banana, peeled and mashed
3 tbsp runny honey
4 tbsp orange juice
200 ml/7 fl oz hand-hot buttermilk
milk, to glaze (optional)
vegetable oil, for brushing

method

1 Place the flour, salt and yeast in a large bowl. Rub in the butter and add the mashed bananas and honey. Make a well in the centre and gradually work in the orange juice and buttermilk to make a smooth dough.

2 Turn the dough out onto a lightly floured work surface and knead for 5–7 minutes, or until the dough is smooth and elastic. If the dough looks very sticky, add a little more white bread flour. (The stickiness depends on the ripeness and size of the bananas.) Place the dough in an oiled bowl, cover with clingfilm and leave in a warm place to rise for 1 hour, or until it has doubled in size.

3 Oil a 900-g/2-lb loaf tin. Turn the dough out onto a lightly floured work surface and knead for 1 minute until smooth. Shape the dough the length of the tin and three times the width. Fold the dough into three lengthways and place it in the tin with the join underneath. Cover and let stand in a warm place for 30 minutes until it has risen above the tin.

4 Just before baking, brush the milk over the loaf to glaze, if using. Bake in a preheated oven, 220ºC/425ºF/Gas Mark 7, for 30 minutes, or until firm and golden brown. Test that the loaf is cooked by tapping it on the bottom – it should sound hollow. Transfer to a wire rack to cool completely before serving.

mango twist bread

ingredients

MAKES 1 LOAF

3 tbsp butter, diced, plus extra for greasing
450 g/1 lb strong white bread flour, plus extra for dusting
1 tsp salt
1 sachet easy-blend dried yeast
1 tsp ground ginger
50 g/1¾ oz brown sugar
1 small mango, peeled, stoned and blended to a purée
250 ml/9 fl oz lukewarm water
2 tbsp honey
125 g/4½ oz sultanas
1 egg, beaten lightly
icing sugar, for dusting

method

1 Grease a baking sheet with a little butter. Sift the flour and salt into a mixing bowl, stir in the dry yeast, ginger and brown sugar and rub in the butter with your fingertips until the mixture resembles breadcrumbs.

2 Stir in the mango purée, lukewarm water and honey and bring together to form a dough.

3 Place the dough on a lightly floured work surface. Knead for about 5 minutes, until smooth. Alternatively, use an electric mixer with a dough hook. Place the dough in a greased bowl, cover and let rise in a warm place for about 1 hour, until it has doubled in size.

4 Knead in the sultanas and shape the dough into 2 rope shapes, each 25 cm/10 inches long. Carefully twist the 2 pieces together and pinch the ends to seal. Place the dough on the baking sheet, cover and let stand in a warm place for a further 40 minutes.

5 Brush the loaf with the egg. Bake in a preheated oven, 220°C/425°F/Gas Mark 7, for 30 minutes, or until golden. Cool on a wire rack and dust with icing sugar before serving.

apricot & walnut bread

ingredients

SERVES 12

55 g/2 oz butter, plus extra for greasing
350 g/12 oz strong white bread flour, plus extra for dusting
1/2 tsp salt
1 tsp golden caster sugar
2 tsp easy-blend dried yeast
115 g/4 oz no-soak dried apricots, chopped
55 g/2 oz chopped walnuts
150 ml/5 fl oz tepid milk
75 ml/2 1/2 fl oz tepid water
1 egg, beaten
vegetable oil, for brushing

topping

85 g/3 oz icing sugar
walnut halves

method

1 Grease and flour a baking sheet. Sift the flour and salt into a warmed bowl and stir in the sugar and yeast. Rub in the butter and add the chopped apricots and walnuts. Make a well in the centre. In a separate bowl, mix together the milk, water and egg. Pour into the dry ingredients and mix to a soft dough. Turn out onto a floured work surface and knead for 10 minutes, or until smooth. Place the dough in a clean bowl brushed with oil, cover with oiled clingfilm and let stand in a warm place for 2–3 hours, or until doubled in size.

2 Turn the dough out onto a floured work surface and knead lightly for 1 minute. Divide into 5 equal pieces and roll each piece into a rope 30 cm/12 inches long. Braid 3 ropes together, pinching the ends to seal, and place on the prepared baking sheet. Twist the remaining 2 ropes together and place on top. Cover lightly with oiled clingfilm and let stand in a warm place for 1–2 hours, or until doubled in size.

3 Bake the bread in a preheated oven, 220°C/425°F/Gas Mark 7, for 10 minutes, then reduce the heat to 190°C/375°F/Gas Mark 5 and bake for a further 20 minutes. Transfer to a wire rack to cool. To make the topping, sift the icing sugar into a bowl, stir in enough water to make a thin icing and drizzle over the loaf. Decorate with walnuts.

crusty white bread

ingredients

MAKES 1 MEDIUM LOAF

1 egg

1 egg yolk

hand-hot water, as required

500 g/1 lb 2 oz white bread flour, plus extra for dusting

$1\frac{1}{2}$ tsp salt

2 tsp sugar

1 tsp easy-blend dried yeast

2 tbsp butter, diced

vegetable oil, for brushing

method

1 Place the egg and egg yolk in a jug and beat lightly to mix. Add enough hand-hot water to make up to 300 ml/10 fl oz. Stir well.

2 Place the flour, salt, sugar and yeast in a large bowl. Add the butter and rub it in with your fingertips until the mixture resembles breadcrumbs. Make a well in the centre, add the egg mixture and work to a smooth dough.

3 Turn the dough out onto a lightly floured work surface and knead for 10 minutes, or until the dough is smooth and elastic. Place the dough in an oiled bowl, cover with clingfilm and let rise in a warm place for 1 hour, or until it has doubled in size.

4 Oil a 900-g/2-lb loaf tin. Turn the dough out onto a lightly floured work surface and knead for 1 minute until smooth. Shape the dough the length of the tin and three times the width. Fold the dough into three lengthways and place it in the tin with the join underneath. Cover and leave in a warm place for 30 minutes until it has risen above the tin.

5 Bake in a preheated oven, 220ºC/425ºF/Gas Mark 7, for 30 minutes, or until firm and golden brown. Test that the loaf is cooked by tapping it on the bottom – it should sound hollow. Transfer to a wire rack to cool completely.

olive & sun-dried tomato bread

ingredients

SERVES 4

400 g/14 oz plain flour, plus extra for dusting
1 tsp salt
1 sachet easy-blend dried yeast
1 tsp brown sugar
1 tbsp chopped fresh thyme
200 ml/7 fl oz warm water (heated to 50°C/122°F)
4 tbsp olive oil, plus extra for oiling
50 g/1$^3/_4$ oz black olives, stoned and sliced
50 g/1$^3/_4$ oz green olives, stoned and sliced
100 g/3$^1/_2$ oz sun-dried tomatoes in oil, drained and sliced
1 egg yolk, beaten

method

1 Place the flour, salt and yeast in a bowl and mix together, then stir in the sugar and thyme. Make a well in the centre. Slowly stir in enough water and oil to make a dough. Mix in the olives and sun-dried tomatoes. Knead the dough for 5 minutes, then form it into a ball. Brush a bowl with oil, add the dough and cover with clingfilm. Let rise in a warm place for about 1$^1/_2$ hours, or until the dough has doubled in size.

2 Dust a baking sheet with flour. Knead the dough lightly, then cut into two halves and shape into ovals or circles. Place them on the baking sheet, cover with clingfilm and let rise again in a warm place for 45 minutes, or until they have doubled in size.

3 Make 3 shallow diagonal cuts on the top of each piece of dough. Brush with the egg. Bake in a preheated oven, 200°C/400°F/ Gas Mark 6, for 40 minutes, or until cooked through – they should be golden on top and sound hollow when tapped on the bottom. Transfer to wire racks to cool. Store in an airtight container for up to 3 days.

black olive focaccia

ingredients

SERVES 12

500 g/1 lb 2 oz strong white bread flour, plus extra for dusting

1 tsp salt

2 tsp easy-blend dried yeast

350 ml/12 fl oz tepid water

6 tbsp extra-virgin olive oil, plus extra for brushing

115 g/4 oz stoned black olives, coarsely chopped

1 tsp rock salt

method

1 Sift the flour and salt into a warmed bowl and stir in the yeast. Pour in the water and 2 tablespoons of the olive oil and mix to a soft dough. Knead the dough on a lightly floured work surface for 5–10 minutes, or until it becomes smooth and elastic. Transfer it to a clean, warmed, oiled bowl and cover with clingfilm. Let stand in a warm place for 1 hour, or until the dough has doubled in size.

2 Brush 2 baking sheets with oil. Punch the dough to knock out the air, then knead on a lightly floured work surface for 1 minute. Add the olives and knead until combined. Divide the dough in half, shape into 2 oval shapes 28 x 23 cm/11 x 9 inches long and place on the prepared baking sheets. Cover with oiled clingfilm and let stand in a warm place for 1 hour, or until the dough is puffy.

3 Press your fingers into the dough to make dimples, drizzle over 2 tablespoons of oil, and sprinkle with the rock salt. Bake in a preheated oven, 200°C/400°F/Gas Mark 6, for 30–35 minutes, or until golden. Drizzle with the remaining olive oil and cover with a cloth, to give a soft crust. Slice each loaf into 6 pieces and serve warm.

focaccia with roasted cherry tomatoes, basil & crispy pancetta

ingredients

SERVES 4–6

500 g/1 lb 2 oz white bread flour, plus extra for kneading and rolling
1 tbsp dried basil
1/2 tsp sugar
2 tsp rapid-rise dried yeast
2 tsp salt
325 ml/11 fl oz lukewarm water
2 tbsp olive oil, plus extra for oiling

topping

400 g/14 oz cherry tomatoes
1 tbsp olive oil, plus extra for oiling and drizzling
200 g/7 oz thick pancetta, diced
4 tbsp chopped fresh basil
salt and pepper

method

1 Place the flour, dried basil, sugar, yeast and salt in a bowl. Combine the water and oil and mix with the dry ingredients to form a soft dough, adding more water if the dough appears too dry. Turn out onto a lightly floured work surface and knead for 10 minutes, until smooth and elastic. Place in a lightly oiled bowl and cover with clingfilm. Let stand in a warm place for 1 hour, or until doubled in size.

2 Place the tomatoes on a baking sheet covered with baking paper, sprinkle with oil and season to taste with salt and pepper. Bake in a preheated oven, 140°C/275°F/ Gas Mark 1, for 30 minutes, until soft.

3 Increase the oven temperature to 220°C/ 425°F/Gas Mark 7. Remove the dough from the bowl and knead again briefly. Shape into a rectangle and place on a lightly oiled baking sheet, turning the dough over to oil both sides. Make rough indentations in the dough using your fingers. Top with the tomatoes and pancetta. Sprinkle with salt and pepper. Let stand in a warm place for 10 minutes for the dough to rise again. Bake for 15–20 minutes, until golden and cooked through. Drizzle with oil and top with fresh basil. Serve warm.

mixed seed bread

ingredients

MAKES 1 MEDIUM LOAF

375 g/13 oz white bread flour, plus extra for dusting
125 g/4½ oz rye flour
1½ tbsp skimmed milk powder
1½ tsp salt
1 tbsp brown sugar
1 tsp easy-blend dried yeast
1½ tbsp sunflower oil
2 tsp lemon juice
300 ml/10 fl oz lukewarm water
1 tsp caraway seeds
½ tsp poppy seeds
½ tsp sesame seeds
vegetable oil, for brushing

topping

1 egg white
1 tbsp water
1 tbsp sunflower or pumpkin seeds

method

1 Place the flours, milk powder, salt, sugar and yeast in a large bowl. Pour in the oil and add the lemon juice and water. Stir in the seeds and mix well to make a smooth dough.

2 Turn the dough out onto a lightly floured work surface and knead for 10 minutes, or until the dough is smooth and elastic. Place the dough in an oiled bowl, cover with clingfilm and let stand in a warm place to rise for 1 hour, or until it has doubled in size.

3 Oil a 900-g/2-lb loaf tin. Turn the dough out onto a lightly floured work surface and knead for 1 minute until smooth. Shape the dough to the length of the tin and three times the width. Fold the dough into three lengthways and place it in the tin with the join underneath. Cover and let stand in a warm place for 30 minutes until it has risen above the tin.

4 For the topping, lightly beat the egg white with the water to make a glaze. Just before baking, brush the glaze over the loaf, then gently press the sunflower or pumpkin seeds all over the top.

5 Bake in a preheated oven, 220°C/425°F/ Gas Mark 7, for 30 minutes, or until firm and golden brown. Test that the loaf is cooked by tapping it on the bottom – it should sound hollow. Transfer to a wire rack to cool completely before serving.

cheese & chive plait

ingredients

SERVES 10

450 g/1 lb strong white bread flour, plus extra for dusting
1 tsp salt
1 tsp caster sugar
1½ tsp easy-blend dried yeast
2 tbsp butter
115 g/4 oz coarsely grated Cheddar cheese
3 tbsp snipped fresh chives
4 spring onions, chopped
150 ml/5 fl oz tepid milk
175 ml/6 fl oz tepid water
vegetable oil, for brushing
beaten egg, for glazing

method

1 Sift the flour and salt into a warmed bowl and stir in the sugar and yeast. Rub in the butter, then stir in the cheese, chives and spring onions. Make a well in the centre. Mix together the milk and water, pour into the well and mix to make a soft dough. Turn the dough out onto a lightly floured work surface and knead for 10 minutes, or until smooth and elastic.

2 Transfer the dough to a clean, oiled bowl and cover with clingfilm. Let stand in a warm place for 1 hour, or until doubled in size. Brush a large baking sheet with oil. Turn the dough out onto a floured work surface and knead for 1 minute. Divide the dough into 3 pieces. Roll out each piece into a rope shape and plait the 3 pieces together, pinching the ends to seal.

3 Place on the prepared baking sheet and cover with oiled clingfilm. Let stand in a warm place for 45 minutes, or until doubled in size. Brush with beaten egg and bake in a preheated oven, 220°C/425°F/Gas Mark 7, for 20 minutes.

4 Reduce the oven temperature to 180°C/350°F/Gas Mark 4 and bake for a further 15 minutes, or until golden brown and the loaf sounds hollow when tapped on the bottom. Serve warm or cold.

english muffins

ingredients

SERVES 10–12

2 x 7-g/1/4-oz sachets easy-blend dried yeast
250 ml/9 fl oz tepid water
125 ml/4 fl oz natural yogurt
450 g/1 lb strong plain flour
1/2 tsp salt
50 g/1 3/4 oz fine semolina
vegetable oil, for greasing
butter and jam (optional), to serve

method

1 Mix the yeast with half the tepid water in a bowl until it has dissolved. Add the remaining water and the yogurt and mix well.

2 Sift the flour into a large bowl and add the salt. Pour in the yeast liquid and mix well to a soft dough. Turn out onto a floured work surface and knead well until very smooth. Put the dough back into the bowl, cover with clingfilm and let rise for 30–40 minutes in a warm place until it has doubled in size.

3 Turn out again onto the work surface and knead lightly. Roll out the dough to a thickness of 2 cm/3/4 inch. Using a 7.5-cm/3-inch cutter, cut into rounds and scatter the semolina over each muffin. Re-roll the trimmings of the dough and make further muffins until it is all used up. Place them on a lightly floured baking sheet, cover and let rise again for 30–40 minutes.

4 Heat a large frying pan and lightly grease with a piece of scrunched-up kitchen paper dipped in vegetable oil. Cook half the muffins for 7–8 minutes on each side, taking care not to burn them. Repeat with the rest of the muffins. Serve at once with lots of butter and jam, if liked.

cheese & tomato pizza

ingredients

SERVES 2

dough

- 225 g/8 oz plain flour, plus extra for dusting
- 1 tsp salt
- 1 tsp easy-blend dried yeast
- 1 tbsp olive oil, plus extra for brushing
- 6 tbsp lukewarm water

topping

- 6 tomatoes, sliced thinly
- 175 g/6 oz mozzarella cheese, drained and sliced thinly
- 2 tbsp shredded fresh basil leaves
- 2 tbsp olive oil
- salt and pepper

method

1 To make the pizza dough, sift the flour and salt into a bowl and stir in the yeast. Make a well in the centre and pour in the oil and water. Gradually incorporate the dry ingredients into the liquid, using a wooden spoon or floured hands.

2 Turn out the dough onto a lightly floured work surface and knead well for 5 minutes, until smooth and elastic. Return to the clean bowl, cover with lightly oiled clingfilm and let rise in a warm place for about 1 hour, or until doubled in size.

3 Turn out the dough onto a lightly floured work surface and knock down. Knead briefly, then cut it in half and roll out each piece into a circle about 5 mm/¼ inch thick. Transfer to a lightly oiled baking sheet and push up the edges with your fingers to form a small rim.

4 For the topping, arrange the tomato and mozzarella slices alternately over the pizza bases. Season to taste with salt and pepper, sprinkle with the basil and drizzle with the olive oil. Bake in a preheated oven, 230°C/450°F/Gas Mark 8, for 15–20 minutes, until the crust is crisp and the cheese has melted. Serve immediately.

blinis

ingredients

SERVES 8

115 g/4 oz buckwheat flour
115 g/4 oz white bread flour
7-g/$^{1}/_{4}$-oz sachet easy-blend dried yeast
1 tsp salt
375 ml/13 fl oz tepid milk
2 eggs, 1 whole and 1 separated
vegetable oil, for brushing
soured cream and smoked salmon, to serve

method

1 Sift both flours into a large, warmed bowl. Stir in the yeast and salt. Beat in the milk, whole egg and egg yolk until smooth. Cover the bowl and let stand in a warm place for 1 hour.

2 Place the egg white in a spotlessly clean bowl and whisk until soft peaks form. Fold into the batter. Brush a heavy-based frying pan with oil and set over medium–high heat. When the frying pan is hot, pour enough of the batter onto the surface to make a blini about the size of a saucer.

3 When bubbles rise, turn the blini over with a spatula and cook the other side until light brown. Wrap in a clean tea towel to keep warm while cooking the remainder. Serve the warm blinis with soured cream and smoked salmon.

savoury nibbles

This chapter has recipes for some really creative and exciting savoury tarts and tartlets, which will please your family and wow your guests at a lunch or supper party; savoury muffins, great for lunchboxes or taking on picnics; and crisp little bites to serve as appetizers with drinks.

Making pastry can be a chore if time is short, so you can use ready-made pastry for the savoury tarts if this is more convenient. However, the Spring Vegetable Tart and the Yellow Courgette Tart have a little Parmesan cheese in the pastry and this really adds a special touch, so try to make this if you can. Tartlets are especially good for serving at a buffet – they are all delicious, and Artichoke & Pancetta, Smoked Salmon, Dill & Horseradish and Feta & Spinach are particularly stylish.

You can pack a lot of goodness into a muffin, so they are great for snacks – Leek & Ham Muffins, Herb Muffins with Smoked Cheese and Soured Cream Muffins with Chives will appeal to younger children, and the others to those with a more sophisticated taste!

Home-baked savoury nibbles are so impressive – serve Spiced Cocktail Bites, Pesto Palmiers or Cheese & Rosemary Sables to get a dinner party off to an excellent start!

triple tomato tart

ingredients

SERVES 6

250 g/9 oz ready-made puff pastry

topping

3 tbsp sun-dried tomato purée
250 g/9 oz ripe vine tomatoes, sliced
150 g/5½ oz cherry tomatoes, cut in half
2 sprigs fresh rosemary
2 tbsp extra virgin olive oil
1 tbsp balsamic vinegar
1 egg yolk
125 g/4½ oz Italian sliced salami, chopped
salt and pepper
handful of thyme sprigs

method

1 Roll out the dough to form a rectangle 35 cm/14 inches long and 25 cm/10 inches wide and lift onto a heavy-duty baking sheet. Spread the sun-dried tomato purée over the dough, leaving a 3-cm/1¼-inch margin round the edge. Arrange the vine tomato slices over the tomato purée, sprinkle over the cherry tomato halves and top with the rosemary. Drizzle with 1 tablespoon of the olive oil and the balsamic vinegar.

2 Brush the edges of the dough with the egg yolk and bake in a preheated oven, 190°C/375°F/Gas Mark 5, for 10 minutes. Sprinkle over the chopped salami and bake for a further 10–15 minutes.

3 Remove the tart from the oven and season to taste with salt and pepper. Drizzle with the remaining olive oil and sprinkle with the thyme.

crab & watercress tart

ingredients

SERVES 6

pastry

125 g/4½ oz plain flour
pinch of salt
75 g/2½ oz cold butter, cut into pieces, plus extra for greasing
cold water

filling

300 g/10½ oz prepared white and brown crabmeat
1 bunch watercress, washed and leaves picked from stems
50 ml/2 fl oz milk
2 large eggs, plus 3 egg yolks
200 ml/7 fl oz double cream
½ tsp ground nutmeg
½ bunch fresh chives, snipped
2 tbsp finely grated Parmesan cheese
salt and pepper
fresh sprigs of watercress, to garnish

method

1 Lightly grease a 23-cm/9-inch loose-based fluted tart tin. Sift the flour and salt into a food processor, add the butter and process until the mixture resembles fine breadcrumbs. Add just enough cold water to bring the dough together.

2 Turn out onto a floured work surface and roll out the dough 8 cm/3¼ inches larger than the tin. Carefully lift the dough into the tin and press to fit. Roll the rolling pin over the tin to neaten the edges and trim the excess dough. Fit a piece of baking paper into the tart case, fill with dried beans and chill in the refrigerator for 30 minutes.

3 Remove the pastry case from the refrigerator and bake blind for 10 minutes in a preheated oven, 190°C/375°F/Gas Mark 5, then remove the beans and paper. Return to the oven for 5 minutes. Remove the tin from the oven and lower the oven temperature to 160°C/325°F/Gas Mark 3.

4 Arrange the crabmeat and watercress in the tart tin. Whisk the milk, eggs and egg yolks together in a bowl. Bring the cream to simmering point in a pan and pour over the egg mixture, whisking all the time. Season with salt, pepper and nutmeg and stir in the chives. Carefully pour this mixture over the crab and watercress and sprinkle over the Parmesan. Bake for 35–40 minutes, until golden and set. Let stand for 10 minutes before serving with sprigs of watercress.

goat's cheese & thyme tart

ingredients

SERVES 6

250 g/9 oz ready-made puff pastry

topping

- 500 g/1 lb 2 oz goat's cheese, such as chèvre, sliced
- 3–4 sprigs fresh thyme, leaves picked from stalks
- 55 g/2 oz black olives, stoned
- 50 g/1¾ oz canned anchovies in olive oil
- 1 tbsp olive oil
- 1 egg yolk
- salt and pepper
- sprigs of fresh thyme, to garnish

method

1 Roll the dough into a large circle or rectangle and place on a baking sheet.

2 Arrange the cheese slices on the dough, leaving a 2.5-cm/1-inch margin round the edge. Sprinkle the thyme and olives, then arrange the anchovies, over the cheese. Drizzle over the olive oil. Season well with salt and pepper and brush the edges of the dough with the egg yolk.

3 Bake in a preheated oven, 190°C/375°F/Gas Mark 5, for 20–25 minutes, until the cheese is bubbling and the pastry is browned. Garnish with sprigs of fresh thyme.

spring vegetable tart

ingredients

SERVES 6

cheese pastry

250 g/9 oz plain flour
pinch of salt
125 g/4½ oz cold butter, cut into pieces
55 g/2 oz grated Parmesan cheese
1 egg
1 tbsp cold water

filling

300 g/11 oz selection of baby spring vegetables, such as carrots, asparagus, peas, broad beans, spring onions, baby corn and leeks, trimmed and peeled where necessary
300 ml/10 fl oz double cream
125 g/4½ oz mature Cheddar cheese, grated
2 eggs plus 3 egg yolks
handful of fresh tarragon and flat-leaf parsley, chopped
salt and pepper

method

1 Grease a 25-cm/10-inch loose-based tart tin. Sift the flour and salt into a food processor, add the butter and pulse to combine, then tip into a large bowl and add the Parmesan cheese. Mix the egg and water together in a small bowl. Add most of the egg mixture and work into a soft dough, using more egg mixture if needed. Turn out onto a floured work surface and roll out the dough 8 cm/3¼ inches larger than the tin. Carefully lift the dough into the tin and press to fit. Roll the rolling pin over the tin to trim the excess dough. Fit a piece of baking paper into the tart case, fill with dried beans and chill in the refrigerator for 30 minutes.

2 Bake the tart case blind for 15 minutes in a preheated oven, 200°C/400°F/Gas Mark 6, then remove the beans and paper and bake for a further 5 minutes. Remove from the oven and cool. Lower the oven temperature to 180°C/350°F/Gas Mark 4.

3 Cut the vegetables into bite-sized pieces and blanch in boiling water. Drain and cool. Bring the cream to simmering point in a pan. Place the cheese, eggs and egg yolks in a heatproof bowl and pour the warm cream over the mixture. Stir to combine, season well and stir in the herbs. Arrange the vegetables in the tart case, pour over the cheese filling and bake for 30–40 minutes, until set. Cool in the tin for 10 minutes before serving.

yellow courgette tart

ingredients

SERVES 6

1 quantity cheese pastry (see page 200)

filling

2 large yellow courgettes
1 tbsp salt
3 heaped tbsp unsalted butter
1 bunch spring onions, trimmed and finely sliced
150 ml/5 fl oz double cream
3 large eggs
1 small bunch of fresh chives, chopped
salt and white pepper

method

1 Grease a 25-cm/10-inch loose-based tart tin. Roll out the pastry 8 cm/3¼ inches larger than the tin. Carefully lift the dough into the tin and press to fit. Roll the rolling pin over the tin to neaten the edges and trim the excess dough. Fit a piece of baking paper into the tart case, fill with dried beans and chill in the refrigerator for 30 minutes.

2 Bake the tart case blind for 15 minutes in a preheated oven, 200°C/400°F/Gas Mark 6, then remove the beans and paper and bake for a further 5 minutes. Remove from the oven and cool. Lower the oven temperature to 180°C/350°F/Gas Mark 4.

3 Meanwhile, grate the courgettes and put in a sieve with 1 tablespoon of salt. Drain for 20 minutes, then rinse and put in a clean tea towel, squeezing all the moisture from the courgettes. Keep dry.

4 Melt the butter in a wide frying pan, sauté the spring onions until soft, then add the courgettes and cook over medium heat for 5 minutes, until any liquid has evaporated. Cool slightly. Whisk the cream and eggs together with the salt and pepper and chives. Spoon the courgettes into the tart case and pour in the cream mixture, making sure it settles properly, then bake for 30 minutes. Serve the tart hot or cold.

squash, sage & gorgonzola tart

ingredients

SERVES 6

1 quantity pastry (see page 196)

filling

$1/2$ small butternut squash or 1 slice pumpkin, weighing 250 g/9 oz
1 tsp olive oil
250 ml/9 fl oz double cream
175 g/6 oz Gorgonzola cheese
2 eggs, plus 1 egg yolk
6–8 fresh sage leaves
salt and pepper

method

1 Cut the squash in half and brush the cut side with the oil. Place cut-side up on a baking sheet and bake for 30–40 minutes, until browned and very soft. Set aside to cool. Remove the seeds and scoop out the flesh into a large bowl, discarding the skin.

2 Lightly grease a 23-cm/9-inch loose-based fluted tart tin. Roll out the pastry 8 cm/ $3^1/4$ inches larger than the tin. Lift the dough into the tin and press to fit. Roll the rolling pin over the tin to trim the excess dough. Fit a piece of baking paper into the tart case and fill it with dried beans. Chill in the refrigerator for 30 minutes, then bake blind for 10 minutes in a preheated oven, 190°C/375°F/Gas Mark 5. Remove the beans and paper and return to the oven for 5 minutes.

3 Mash the squash and mix it with half the cream, season with salt and pepper, then spread it in the pastry case. Slice the cheese and lay it on top. Whisk the remaining cream with the eggs and egg yolk and pour the mixture into the tart tin, making sure it settles evenly. Arrange the sage leaves in a circle on the surface. Bake for 30–35 minutes and leave for 10 minutes in the tin before serving.

artichoke & pancetta tartlets

ingredients

SERVES 6

1 quantity pastry (see page 196)

filling

5 tbsp double cream
4 tbsp bottled artichoke paste
400 g/14 oz canned artichoke hearts, drained
12 thin-cut pancetta slices
rocket leaves
50 g/1¾ oz Parmesan or pecorino cheese
2 tbsp olive oil, for drizzling
salt and pepper

method

1 Grease 6 x 9-cm/3½-inch loose-based fluted tart tins. Divide the pastry into 6 pieces. Roll each piece to fit the tart tins. Carefully fit each piece of dough in its tin and press well to fit. Roll the rolling pin over the tin to trim the excess dough. Cut 6 pieces of baking paper and fit a piece into each tart, fill with dried beans and chill in the refrigerator for 30 minutes.

2 Bake the tart cases for 10 minutes in a preheated oven, 200°C/400°F/Gas Mark 6, and then remove the beans and baking paper.

3 Meanwhile, stir the cream and the artichoke paste together and season well with salt and pepper. Divide between the pastry cases, spreading out to cover the base of each tart. Cut each artichoke heart into 3 pieces and divide between the tarts, curl 2 slices of the pancetta into each tart and bake for 10 minutes.

4 To serve, top each tart with a good amount of rocket then, using a potato peeler, sprinkle shavings of the Parmesan cheese over the tarts, drizzle with olive oil and serve at once.

smoked salmon, dill & horseradish tartlets

ingredients

SERVES 6

1 quantity pastry (see page 196)

filling

125 ml/4 fl oz soured cream
1 tsp creamed horseradish
½ tsp lemon juice
1 tsp Spanish capers, chopped
3 egg yolks
200 g/7 oz smoked salmon trimmings
bunch fresh dill, chopped
salt and pepper

method

1 Grease 6 x 9-cm/3½-inch loose-based fluted tart tins. Divide the pastry into 6 pieces. Roll each piece to fit the tart tins. Carefully fit each piece of dough in its tin and press well to fit. Roll the rolling pin over the tin to trim the excess dough. Cut 6 pieces of baking paper and fit a piece into each tart, fill with dried beans and chill in the refrigerator for 30 minutes.

2 Bake the tart cases for 10 minutes in a preheated oven, 200°C/400°F/Gas Mark 6, and then remove the beans and baking paper.

3 Meanwhile, put the soured cream, horseradish, lemon juice, capers and salt and pepper into a bowl and mix well. Add the egg yolks, the smoked salmon and the dill and carefully mix again. Divide this mixture between the tart cases and return to the oven for 10 minutes. Cool in the tins for 5 minutes before serving.

blue cheese & walnut tartlets

ingredients

SERVES 12

pastry

250 g/9 oz plain flour

pinch of celery salt

100 g/3½ oz cold butter, cut into pieces, plus extra for greasing

40 g/1½ oz walnut halves, chopped in a food processor

cold water

filling

2 tbsp butter

2 celery stalks, trimmed and finely chopped

1 small leek, trimmed and finely chopped

200 ml/7 fl oz double cream, plus 2 tbsp extra

200 g/7 oz blue cheese

3 egg yolks

salt and pepper

chopped fresh parsley, to garnish

method

1 Lightly grease a 7.5-cm/3-inch, 12-cup muffin tin. Sift the flour and celery salt into a food processor, add the butter and process until the mixture resembles fine breadcrumbs. Tip the mixture into a bowl. Add the walnuts and enough cold water to bring the dough together.

2 Turn out onto a floured work surface and cut the dough in half. Roll out the first piece and cut out 6 x 9-cm/3½-inch circles. Roll out each circle to a 12-cm/4½-inch diameter and press into the muffin cups. Repeat with the remaining dough. Put a piece of baking paper in each cup and fill with dried beans. Chill in the refrigerator for 30 minutes, then bake blind for 10 minutes in a preheated oven, 200°C/400°F/Gas Mark 6. Remove the paper and beans.

3 Melt the butter in a frying pan, add the celery and leek and cook for 15 minutes, until soft. Add 2 tablespoons of double cream and crumble in the blue cheese. Mix well and season to taste. Bring the remaining cream to simmering point in a pan, then pour onto the egg yolks, stirring. Mix in the blue cheese mixture and spoon into the pastry cases. Bake for 10 minutes, then turn the tin round in the oven and bake for a further 5 minutes. Cool in the tin for 5 minutes and sprinkle with parsley.

feta & spinach tartlets

ingredients

SERVES 6

1 quantity pastry (see page 196) with 1/2 nutmeg, freshly grated, added to the flour

filling

225 g/8 oz baby spinach
2 tbsp butter
150 ml/5 fl oz double cream
3 egg yolks
125 g/4 1/2 oz feta cheese
25 g/1 oz pine nuts
salt and pepper
cherry tomatoes and sprigs of flat-leaf parsley, to garnish

method

1 Grease 6 x 9-cm/3 1/2-inch loose-based fluted tart tins. Divide the pastry into 6 pieces. Roll each piece to fit the tart tins. Carefully fit each piece of dough in its tin and press well to fit. Roll the rolling pin over the tin to trim the excess dough. Cut 6 pieces of baking paper and fit a piece into each tart, then fill with dried beans and chill in the refrigerator for 30 minutes.

2 Bake the tart cases for 10 minutes in a preheated oven, 200°C/400°F/Gas Mark 6, and then remove the beans and baking paper.

3 Blanch the spinach in boiling water for just 1 minute, then drain and press to squeeze all the water out. Chop the spinach. Melt the butter in a frying pan, add the spinach and cook gently to evaporate any remaining liquid. Season well with salt and pepper. Stir in the cream and egg yolks. Crumble the feta and divide between the tarts, top with the creamed spinach and bake for 10 minutes. Sprinkle the pine nuts over the tartlets and cook for a further 5 minutes. Garnish with cherry tomatoes and sprigs of flat-leaf parsley.

cherry tomato & poppy seed tartlets

ingredients

SERVES 12

pastry

200 g/7 oz plain flour
pinch of salt
100 g/3½ oz cold butter, cut into pieces
2 tsp poppy seeds
cold water

filling

24 cherry tomatoes
1 tbsp olive oil
2 tbsp unsalted butter
2 tbsp plain flour
250 ml/9 fl oz milk
50 g/1¾ oz mature Cheddar cheese
100 g/3½ oz cream cheese
salt and pepper
12 fresh basil leaves, to garnish

method

1 Lightly grease a 7.5-cm/3-inch, 12-cup muffin tin. Sift the flour and salt into a food processor, add the butter and process until the mixture resembles fine breadcrumbs. Tip the mixture into a large bowl and add the poppy seeds and just enough cold water to bring the dough together.

2 Turn out onto a floured work surface and cut the dough in half. Roll out the first piece and cut out 6 x 9-cm/3½-inch circles. Roll out each circle to a 12-cm/4½-inch diameter and press into the muffin cups. Repeat with the remaining dough. Put a piece of baking paper in each cup and fill with dried beans. Chill in the refrigerator for 30 minutes. Bake blind for 10 minutes in a preheated oven, 200°C/400°F/Gas Mark 6, then remove the paper and beans.

3 Put the tomatoes in an ovenproof dish, drizzle with the olive oil and roast for 5 minutes.

4 Melt the butter in a pan, stir in the flour and cook for 5–8 minutes. Gradually add the milk, stirring, and cook for a further 5 minutes. Season well and stir in the cheeses until well combined. Put 2 tomatoes in each tart case and spoon in the cheese sauce, then put back into the oven for 15 minutes. Remove from the oven and top each tartlet with a basil leaf.

aubergine & pesto tartlets

ingredients

SERVES 6

250 g/9 oz ready-made puff pastry

filling

1 large or 2 small aubergines, trimmed and thinly sliced
5 tbsp olive oil
3 buffalo mozzarella cheeses, sliced
6 tbsp pesto
pepper
1 egg yolk

method

1 Roll out the puff pastry on a lightly floured work surface and divide into 6 pieces. Roll each piece into either circles or rectangles, then place on 2 baking sheets, 3 on each.

2 Brush the aubergine slices with 2 tablespoons of the olive oil and cook briefly in a non-stick frying pan, in batches, then arrange the slices neatly overlapping on each dough base, leaving a 2.5-cm/1-inch margin round the edges. Lay the mozzarella slices over the aubergine slices and spoon over the pesto. Drizzle with the remaining olive oil and season with pepper.

3 Brush the edges of the dough with egg yolk and bake in a preheated oven, 190°C/375°F/ Gas Mark 5, for 15 minutes. Remove from the oven and serve.

spicy chicken muffins

ingredients

SERVES 12

125 ml/4 fl oz sunflower or groundnut oil, plus extra for oiling
2 onions, chopped
3 spring onions, chopped
1 small fresh red chilli, seeded and finely chopped
3 skinless, boneless chicken thighs, chopped into small pieces
1 tsp paprika
300 g/10½ oz self-raising flour
1 tsp baking powder
2 large eggs
1 tbsp lemon juice
1 tbsp grated lemon rind
125 ml/4 fl oz soured cream
125 ml/4 fl oz plain yogurt
salt and pepper

method

1 Oil a 12-cup muffin tin with sunflower oil. Heat a little of the remaining oil in a frying pan, add the onions, spring onions and chilli and cook over low heat, stirring constantly, for 3 minutes. Remove from the heat, lift out the onions and chilli and set aside. Heat a little more of the remaining oil in the frying pan, add the chicken and paprika and cook, stirring, over medium heat for 5 minutes. Remove from the heat and set aside.

2 Sift the flour and baking powder into a large mixing bowl. In a separate bowl, lightly beat the eggs, then stir in the remaining oil and the lemon juice and rind. Pour in the soured cream and the yogurt and mix together. Add the egg mixture to the flour mixture, then gently stir in the onions, spring onions, chilli and chicken. Season to taste with salt and pepper. Do not overstir the batter – it is fine for it to be a little lumpy.

3 Divide the muffin batter evenly between the 12 cups in the muffin tin (they should reach the top), then transfer to a preheated oven, 190°C/375°F/Gas Mark 5. Bake for 20 minutes, or until risen and golden. Remove the muffins from the oven and serve warm, or place them on a wire rack to cool.

savoury leek & ham muffins

ingredients

SERVES 12

2 tbsp sunflower or groundnut oil, plus extra for oiling (if using)
1 leek, washed, trimmed and finely chopped
280 g/10 oz plain flour
2 tsp baking powder
1/2 tsp bicarbonate of soda
1 large egg, lightly beaten
300 ml/10 fl oz thick strained plain yogurt
4 tbsp butter, melted
25 g/1 oz Cheddar cheese, grated
25 g/1 oz fresh chives, finely snipped
150 g/5 1/2 oz cooked ham, chopped

method

1 Oil a 12-cup muffin tin with sunflower oil, or line it with 12 muffin paper liners. Heat the remaining oil in a frying pan, add the chopped leek and cook, stirring, over low heat for 2 minutes. Remove from the heat and cool.

2 Sift the flour, baking powder and bicarbonate of soda into a large mixing bowl. In a separate bowl, lightly mix the egg, yogurt and melted butter together. Add the Cheddar cheese, chives, cooked leek and half of the chopped ham, then mix together well. Add the cheese mixture to the flour mixture, then gently stir together until just combined. Do not overstir the batter – it is fine for it to be a little lumpy.

3 Divide the muffin batter evenly between the 12 cups in the muffin tin or the paper liners (they should be about two-thirds full). Sprinkle over the remaining chopped ham, then transfer to a preheated oven, 200°C/400°F/Gas Mark 6. Bake for 20 minutes, or until risen and golden. Remove the muffins from the oven and serve warm, or place them on a wire rack to cool.

potato & pancetta muffins

ingredients

SERVES 12

1 tbsp sunflower or groundnut oil, plus extra for oiling (if using)
3 shallots, finely chopped
350 g/12 oz self-raising flour
1 tsp salt
450 g/1 lb potatoes, cooked and mashed
2 large eggs
350 ml/12 fl oz milk
125 ml/4 fl oz soured cream
1 tbsp finely snipped fresh chives
150 g/5½ oz pancetta, grilled and crumbled into pieces
4 tbsp grated Cheddar cheese

method

1 Oil a 12-cup muffin tin with sunflower oil, or line it with 12 muffin paper liners. Heat the remaining oil in a frying pan, add the chopped shallots and cook, stirring, over low heat for 2 minutes. Remove from the heat and cool.

2 Sift the flour and salt into a large mixing bowl. In a separate bowl, mix together the mashed potatoes, eggs, milk, soured cream, chives and half of the pancetta. Add the potato mixture to the flour mixture and then gently stir together until just combined. Do not overstir the batter – it is fine for it to be a little lumpy.

3 Divide the muffin batter evenly between the 12 cups in the muffin tin or the paper liners (they should be about two-thirds full). Sprinkle over the remaining pancetta, then sprinkle over the grated Cheddar cheese. Transfer to a preheated oven, 200°C/400°F/Gas Mark 6, and bake for 20 minutes, or until risen and golden. Remove the muffins from the oven and serve warm, or place them on a wire rack to cool.

crab & cream cheese muffins

ingredients

SERVES 12

1 tbsp sunflower or groundnut oil, for oiling (if using)
280 g/10 oz plain flour
1½ tsp baking powder
½ tsp bicarbonate of soda
½ tsp salt
1 large egg
150 ml/5 fl oz plain yogurt
150 ml/5 fl oz soured cream
25 g/1 oz Cheddar cheese, grated
25 g/1 oz chopped fresh parsley
25 g/1 oz chopped fresh dill

crab & cream cheese filling

200 g/7 oz canned crabmeat, drained
225 g/8 oz cream cheese
2 tbsp mayonnaise
salt and pepper

method

1 Oil a 12-cup muffin tin with sunflower oil, or line it with 12 muffin paper liners. Sift the flour, baking powder, bicarbonate of soda and salt into a large mixing bowl.

2 In a separate bowl, lightly beat the egg, then mix in the yogurt and soured cream. Stir in the grated cheese and chopped herbs. Add the soured cream and cheese mixture to the flour mixture and stir in gently. Do not overstir the batter – it is fine for it to be a little lumpy.

3 Divide the muffin batter evenly between the 12 cups in the muffin tin or the paper liners (they should be about two-thirds full), then transfer to a preheated oven, 200°C/400°F/Gas Mark 6. Bake for 20 minutes, or until risen and golden.

4 Meanwhile, make the filling. Place the crabmeat in a mixing bowl and flake with a fork. Add the cream cheese and mayonnaise, mix together well and season to taste. Cover the bowl with clingfilm and chill.

5 Transfer the cooked muffins to a wire rack and cool to room temperature. Cut them in half horizontally. Spread the crabmeat filling over the bottom halves of the muffins. Replace the top halves, so that the filling is sandwiched in the middle, and serve.

herb muffins with smoked cheese

ingredients

SERVES 12

1 tbsp sunflower or groundnut oil, for oiling (if using)
280 g/10 oz plain flour
2 tsp baking powder
1/2 tsp bicarbonate of soda
25 g/1 oz smoked hard cheese, grated
50 g/1 3/4 oz fresh parsley, finely chopped
1 large egg, lightly beaten
300 ml/10 fl oz thick strained plain yogurt
4 tbsp butter, melted

method

1 Oil a 12-cup muffin tin with sunflower oil, or line it with 12 muffin paper liners. Sift the flour, baking powder and bicarbonate of soda into a large mixing bowl. Add the smoked cheese and the parsley and mix together well.

2 In a separate bowl, lightly mix the egg, yogurt and melted butter together. Add the yogurt mixture to the flour mixture and then gently stir together until just combined. Do not overstir the batter – it is fine for it to be a little lumpy.

3 Divide the muffin batter evenly between the 12 cups in the muffin tin or the paper liners (they should be about two-thirds full), then transfer to a preheated oven, 200°C/400°F/Gas Mark 6. Bake for 20 minutes, or until risen and golden. Remove the muffins from the oven and serve warm, or place them on a wire rack to cool.

soured cream muffins with chives

ingredients

SERVES 12

1 tbsp sunflower or groundnut oil, for oiling (if using)
280 g/10 oz plain flour
2 tsp baking powder
1/2 tsp bicarbonate of soda
25 g/1 oz Cheddar cheese, grated
35 g/1 1/4 oz fresh chives, finely snipped, plus extra to garnish
1 large egg, lightly beaten
200 ml/7 fl oz soured cream
100 ml/3 1/2 fl oz plain unsweetened yogurt
4 tbsp butter, melted

method

1 Oil a 12-cup muffin tin with sunflower oil, or line it with 12 muffin paper liners. Sift the flour, baking powder and bicarbonate of soda into a large mixing bowl. Add the cheese and chives and mix together well.

2 In a separate bowl, lightly mix the egg, soured cream, yogurt and melted butter together. Add the soured cream mixture to the flour mixture and then gently stir together until just combined. Do not overstir the batter – it is fine for it to be a little lumpy.

3 Divide the muffin batter evenly between the 12 cups in the muffin tin or the paper liners (they should be about two-thirds full). Sprinkle over the remaining snipped chives to garnish and transfer to a preheated oven, 200°C/400°F/Gas Mark 6. Bake for 20 minutes, or until risen and golden. Remove the muffins from the oven and serve warm, or place them on a wire rack to cool.

spiced cocktail bites

ingredients

SERVES ABOUT 20

- 115 g/4 oz butter, plus extra for greasing
- 140 g/5 oz plain flour, plus extra for dusting
- 2 tsp curry powder
- 85 g/3 oz grated Cheddar cheese
- 2 tsp poppy seeds
- 1 tsp black onion seeds
- 1 egg yolk
- cumin seeds, for sprinkling

method

1 Grease 2 baking sheets with a little butter. Sift the flour and curry powder into a bowl. Cut the butter into pieces and add to the flour. Rub in until the mixture resembles breadcrumbs, then stir in the cheese, poppy seeds and black onion seeds. Stir in the egg yolk and mix to a firm dough.

2 Wrap the dough in clingfilm and chill in the refrigerator for 30 minutes. On a floured work surface, roll out the dough to 3 mm/1/8 inch thick. Stamp out shapes with a cutter. Re-roll the trimmings and stamp out more shapes until the dough is used up.

3 Place the biscuits on the prepared baking sheets and sprinkle with the cumin seeds. Chill for a further 15 minutes. Bake in a preheated oven, 190°C/375°F/Gas Mark 5, for 20 minutes, or until crisp and golden. Serve warm or transfer to wire racks to cool.

savoury curried bites

ingredients

SERVES 40

100 g/3½ oz butter, softened, plus extra for greasing
100 g/3½ oz plain flour, plus extra for dusting
1 tsp salt
2 tsp curry powder
100 g/3½ oz grated mature Cheddar cheese
100 g/3½ oz freshly grated Parmesan cheese

method

1 Lightly grease about 4 baking sheets with a little butter.

2 Sift the flour and salt into a mixing bowl. Stir in the curry powder and both the grated cheeses. Rub in the softened butter with your fingertips, then bring the mixture together to form a soft dough.

3 Roll out the dough thinly on a lightly floured work surface to form a rectangle. Cut out 40 circles using a 5-cm/2-inch biscuit cutter and arrange on the baking sheets. Bake in a preheated oven, 180°C/350°F/Gas Mark 4, for 10–15 minutes, until golden brown.

4 Let the biscuits cool slightly on the baking sheets, then transfer them to a wire rack to cool completely and crispen.

pesto palmiers

ingredients

SERVES 20

butter, for greasing
plain flour, for dusting
250 g/9 oz ready-made puff pastry
3 tbsp green or red pesto
1 egg yolk, beaten with 1 tbsp water
25 g/1 oz freshly grated Parmesan cheese
sprigs of fresh basil, to garnish

method

1 Grease a baking sheet with a little butter. On a floured work surface, roll out the pastry to a 35 x 15-cm/14 x 6-inch rectangle and trim the edges with a sharp knife. Spread the pesto evenly over the pastry. Roll up the ends tightly to meet in the centre of the pastry.

2 Wrap in clingfilm and chill in the refrigerator for 20 minutes, until firm, then remove from the refrigerator and unwrap. Brush with the beaten egg yolk on all sides. Cut across into 1-cm/½-inch thick slices. Place the slices on the prepared baking sheet.

3 Bake in a preheated oven, 200°C/400°F/ Gas Mark 6, for 10 minutes, or until crisp and golden. Remove from the oven and immediately sprinkle over the Parmesan cheese. Serve the palmiers warm or transfer to a wire rack and cool to room temperature. Garnish with sprigs of fresh basil.

cheese straws

ingredients

SERVES 24

115 g/4 oz plain flour, plus extra for dusting
pinch of salt
1 tsp curry powder
55 g/2 oz butter, plus extra for greasing
55 g/2 oz grated Cheddar cheese
1 egg, beaten
poppy and cumin seeds, for sprinkling

method

1 Sift the flour, salt and curry powder into a bowl. Add the butter and rub in until the mixture resembles breadcrumbs. Add the cheese and half the egg and mix to form a dough. Wrap in clingfilm and chill in the refrigerator for 30 minutes.

2 Lightly grease several baking sheets. On a floured work surface, roll out the dough to 5-mm/1/4-inch thick. Cut into 7.5 x 1-cm/ 3 x 1/2-inch strips. Pinch the strips lightly along the sides and place on the prepared baking sheets.

3 Brush the straws with the remaining egg and sprinkle half with poppy seeds and half with cumin seeds. Bake in a preheated oven, 200°C/400°F/Gas Mark 6, for 10–15 minutes, or until golden. Transfer to wire racks to cool.

cheese & rosemary sables

ingredients

SERVES 40

225 g/8 oz cold butter, diced, plus extra for greasing
250 g/9 oz plain flour
250 g/9 oz grated Gruyère cheese
1/2 tsp cayenne pepper
2 tsp finely chopped fresh rosemary leaves
1 egg yolk, beaten with 1 tbsp water

method

1 Lightly grease 2 baking sheets. Place the flour, butter, cheese, cayenne pepper and chopped rosemary in a food processor. Pulse until the mixture forms a dough, adding a little cold water, if necessary, to bring the mixture together.

2 On a floured work surface, roll out the dough to 5 mm/1/4 inch thick. Stamp out shapes such as stars and hearts with 6-cm/2 1/2-inch biscuit cutters.

3 Place the shapes on the prepared baking sheets, then cover with clingfilm and chill in the refrigerator for 30 minutes, or until firm. Brush with the beaten egg yolk and bake in a preheated oven, 180°C/350°F/Gas Mark 4, for 10 minutes, or until golden brown. Cool on the baking sheets for 2 minutes, then serve warm or transfer to wire racks to cool.